Serving Them Right

SERVING THEM RIGHT

Innovative and Powerful Customer Retention Strategies

Laura A. Liswood

1817

HARPER BUSINESS
A Division of Harper & Row, Publishers, New York

Grand Rapids, Philadelphia, St. Louis, San Francisco
London, Singapore, Sydney, Tokyo, Toronto

International Standard Book Number: 0-88730-346-3

Library of Congress Catalog Card Number: 89-26701

Printed in the United States of America

Library of Congress Cataloging-in-Publication Data

Liswood, Laura A., 1950-
    Serving them right : innovative and powerful customer retention strategies/Laura A. Liswood.
        p.   cm.
    ISBN 0-88730-346-3
    1. Customer service—United States.   2. Customer satisfaction—United States.   I. Title.
HF5415.5.L57   1990
658.8'12—dc20   89-26701
                                                        CIP

90 91 92 93 HC 9 8 7 6 5 4 3 2 1

To my parents, Steve and Dorothy.
They had faith in me from the beginning.
And to my grandparents, Slim and Lillian,
whose way of love and life in Taos
has always been a model.

CONTENTS

Foreword

We at Bain & Company believe that customer retention is one of the most important strategic issues for the 1990s. Our research has shown that it is the key to driving profits and competitiveness. We have found that most senior executives realize they must better serve and retain their customers, but they have been frustrated in their ability to manage their organizations toward superior *profitability* through improvements in service quality.

We have spent the last two years researching customer retention issues with some of the leading business school academics. We have also field-tested the work with *dramatic* results. In businesses as diverse as banking, software, distribution, health care, insurance broking, retailing, and automotive service, our work has shown that a 5 percent change in the rate of retention swings profits from 25 to 100 percent. Business people cannot afford to just shrug their shoulders.

There is a real need for continued development in the area of customer retention because the manufacturing quality revolution of the past decade has barely touched

the service sector. In manufacturing, companies found
that the key to the revolution was their ability to calculate the economics of quality. Following the lead of
manufacturing companies, some service companies have
attempted to force-fit the same tools with unimpressive
results. The fact is that these frameworks don't apply to
service businesses.

In a service business (or in the service components of
a manufacturing business) the best measure of quality
and value is customer retention. And we now know that
customer retention is the link between quality and profits.

In services, we have learned that an error is not necessarily a defect. In fact, there is strong evidence that if
an error is corrected effectively, customer loyalty actually
increases. The breakthrough insight in service is that if
the customer keeps coming back and gives you all of his
or her business, then you have met the customer's quality
standards. Rather than managing defects in service, one
manages *defections*.

Defections have a cost that can be calculated. This
means that a manager can evaluate and act upon the
economics of service quality. For example, a $10 mil-
lion investment in a superior telephone-answering system must be justified by a specific reduction in defections
that can be evaluated. This unleashes the power of economic investment analysis through standard tools such as
breakeven analysis, payback, rate of return, and net pre-
sent value, and clears the path for the steady, incremental
improvements that formed the basis for the manufacturing quality revolution.

Our research shows that firms vastly underestimate the
cost of losing a customer. Very few even track defections,
let alone invest in reducing them. Laura Liswood has said:
"Ask a bank branch manager 'how many new accounts did
you open last month?' and he will know the answer. Ask
'how many accounts did you lose?' and he will shrug his
shoulders."

Given the overwhelming economic impact of retention—a 5 percent change in retention swinging profits

from 25 to 100 percent—it is clear that companies *must* determine the reason for each and every defection and take appropriate action. Once managers understand the economics of defections, we believe they will conclude that the most profitable target will approximate zero. That is why we call our program of management tools Zero Defections℠.

Senior management commitment is a must in working towards Zero Defections℠—but it is not enough. Companies must reorient their information systems, incentives, training, hiring, complaint handling, organizational structure, and culture. They must make customer retention their primary performance measure—not just a measure for error and complaint-handling and customer feedback programs, but the guiding principle for strategic decisions and investment policies.

Serving Them Right: Innovative and Powerful Customer Retention Strategies embraces many of the concepts and principles that we have found to be important to our clients as they aim toward Zero Defections℠. Laura Liswood gives practical advice for all levels of an organization, including provocative, new ideas such as the need for a chief service officer, a complete realignment of complaint handling by top management, and a new set of service measurement standards. We believe these are worthy of consideration and representative of the types of changes that senior managers must make. The picture is not grim—in fact, the opportunity for improved results will be extraordinary throughout the 1990s as managers come to realize the strategic implications of customer retention.

Fred Reichheld
Customer Retention Practice Leader
Bain & Company

Preface

THE MALCOLM Baldrige National Quality Awards were given out in November 1989 to two major American companies. This represents the second year the awards have been given. The Award is given to no more than six companies who have been recognized as the best organizations in quality in the United States. The criteria for the award are substantive, comprehensive, and well-defined. There are several hundred criteria structured to evaluate every element and person within an organization. These criteria alone practically define what world-class quality means.

In 1989, 40 companies applied for awards. Of these, 23 were in manufacturing, 11 in small business, and six in service. Ten companies, eight in manufacturing and two in service, were site visited. The two 1989 winners were Milliken and Company and Xerox Corporation's Business Products and Systems.

Again, this year no service company won an award. Many of the applicants in the small business and service categories appear to be moving toward total quality systems.

The award requires competitive and trend data, which may be more familiar and obtainable in manufacturing companies. The examiners concluded that, as yet, service companies lack sufficient transferable strategies and demonstrable results to warrant awards.

The winners and site-visit candidates exhibit similar traits and characteristics:

1. Quality is a way to differentiate yourself in the market; it is a basis for market share growth.

2. Quality is the preferred route to productivity gains. Fifteen to forty percent productivity advantages have been documented.

3. Strong leadership is the crucial ingredient to create and sustain a quality culture. The leadership must completely embrace the quality process in everything it and its organization does.

4. The quality of leading companies depends in large part on the quality of the suppliers. The best companies are now limiting their business to suppliers that meet demanding quality requirements. Robert Galvin, the chairman of Motorola, a 1988 Quality Award winner, has decreed that all of his suppliers should be applicants for the award within five years.

5. Training and education are major investments for leading companies. A significant dollar investment is required for basic skills teaching.

6. Leading companies do not just compare themselves with the local competition but derive their standing and methods by studying the successes of companies around the world.

7. These companies have confirmed the correlation between worker satisfaction and customer satisfaction. They give workers more responsibility and authority, thereby contributing to reduced turnover, absenteeism, and accidents.

Milliken and Company — 1989 National Quality Award Winner

Ten years ago, Milliken and Company, a major textile manufacturer long-recognized for quality products and its use of state-of-the-art technology, asked why some Japanese competitors achieved higher quality, less waste, greater productivity, and fewer customer complaints while using technology less advanced than their own. The reasons, company executives found, lay in management approaches and in personal practices that, along with technology, drive improvements in quality and efficiency.

In 1981, senior management set in motion Milliken's Pursuit of Excellence (POE) program, a commitment to customer satisfaction that pervades all company levels at all locations. The results are impressive, providing improvements in what has already been an enviable record of quality and performance. In independently conducted surveys, Milliken tops the competition in all 15 measures of customer satisfaction.

For the South Carolina-based company, the wisdom of a "customer-driven and quality-focused" approach to manufacturing and nonmanufacturing activities is verified by its business success. Since the early 1980s, productivity has increased 42 percent and sales have risen dramatically.

Milliken at a Glance

Headquartered in Spartanburg, South Carolina, the 124-year-old privately owned company employs 14,300 workers (whom the company terms "associates") most at Milliken's 47 facilities in the United States. Its 28 businesses produce more than 48,000 different textile and chemical products—ranging from apparel fabrics to specialty chemicals and floor coverings—for more than 8,500 customers worldwide. Annual sales exceed $1 billion.

Milliken's successful push for quality improvement has

allowed it to increase it domestic sales even as imports
threaten the U.S. textile industry. Not yielding to foreign
competitors at home, Milliken is also prospering overseas.
Its automotive fabrics business, for example, is now a
major supplier of high-quality upholstery to Japanese and
Korean car manufacturers.

Pursuit of Excellence

Commitment to quality and customer satisfaction begins
at the company's highest levels, with Roger Milliken, chief
executive officer, and Thomas J. Malone, chief operating
officer, devoting more than half their time to Milliken's
POE process.

Through the Policy Committee and Quality Council, top
management creates the environment and provides the
leadership for quality improvement, and it closely monitors the progress of each company unit toward quality
goals.

Milliken has achieved a flat management structure
in which associates, working primarily in self-managed
teams, exercise considerable authority and autonomy.
Production work teams, for example, can undertake training, schedule work, and establish individual performance
objectives. Moreover, any of Milliken's associates can halt
a production process if that person detects a quality or
safety problem.

This approach has worked so well that Milliken has
reduced the number of management positions by nearly
700 since 1981, freeing up a large portion of the workforce
for assignment as process improvement specialists. There
has been a 77-percent increase in the ratio of production
to management associates.

Teams are a hallmark of what observers now call the
Milliken Quality Process. In 1988, 1,600 Corrective Action
Teams were formed to address specific manufacturing or
other internal business challenges, and about 200 Supplier Action Teams worked to improve Milliken's relationships with its suppliers. In addition, nearly 500 Cus-

tomer Action Teams were formed to respond to the needs and aims of customers, including development of new products. Besides demonstrating a commitment to customer satisfaction, these teams created marketing opportunities that generated substantial additional sales revenue.

Complementing its many activities to extend the capabilities of its workforce, Milliken invests heavily in training. The company spent about $1,300 per associate in 1988. Training is also extended to Milliken's suppliers and customers. Each year since 1984, more than 7,500 visitors have received training in quality principles at Milliken's dedicated training facilities.

The recognition process, for both teams and individuals, is a highly visible, motivating force throughout the company. Participation by senior leadership is commonplace and extensive. Supplier recognition activities are a natural extension of those used within the company.

All the quality improvement efforts are solidly based on information contained in an array of standardized databases accessible from all Milliken facilities. Most manufacturing processes are under the scrutiny of real-time monitoring systems that detect errors and help pinpoint causes. The resultant data, some analyzed with the aid of computerized expert systems, support process improvement efforts to predict and prevent the causes of errors.

To speed progress in this area, process improvement specialists—the reassigned production managers—analyze and improve processes, including those in such nonmanufacturing areas as billing and customer service. A substantial decrease in errors has been realized. Since 1981, a 60 percent reduction has been effected in the cost of nonconformance, which includes discounts for off quality, payment for freight on customer returns, and other cost items.

Milliken also maintains extensive databases on environmental and safety variables, suppliers, and customers, including the results of its extensive annual surveys on customer satisfaction. In addition, the company "bench-marks" the products and services of about 400 competi-tors, providing concrete measures for assessing its perfor-mance and for identifying market opportunities.

Through this surveillance, Milliken determined, for example, that it trailed some competitors in meeting delivery targets. As a result, Milliken improved its record for on-time delivery from 75 percent in 1984 to an indus-try best of 99 percent in 1988.

Suppliers play an important role in Milliken's quality success. Through extensive efforts in developing supplier partnerships, the company has been able to reduce the number of its suppliers by 72 percent since 1981.

Customer Responsiveness

A key element of Milliken's approach to quality is cus-tomer responsiveness—providing what its customers need when they need it. Advanced technology developed by Milliken provides customer access to the company's state-of-the-art computer automated design, which dramati-cally reduces the cycle time for new product development. Another critical element for textile users is the time to deliver sample material. Milliken's performance is con-sidered the best in the textile business.

Roger Milliken has personally played a key role in pio-neering quick response as an important strategy for Amer-ican industry.

The company has been well-recognized for achieving success for its customers. Milliken has received 41 major customer quality awards in the past five years, including a record number of General Motors Mark of Excellence awards. In addition, Milliken was voted the outstanding residential carpet manufacturer in the United States in 1988.

At Milliken, the Pursuit of Excellence is an evolving process that continually yields new ideas for enhancing quality, increasing customer satisfaction, and improving business performance. Building on its quality successes,

Milliken has established ambitious new objectives, called "Ten-Four" objectives, as a focus for future advances.

The Company intends to achieve tenfold improvement in key, customer-focused quality measures over the next four years. Each advance brings the innovative company closer to its long-range goal of a production system that is fully responsive to customer needs, providing, as Milliken says, "products that customers want, in the quantity they want, when they want them."

Source: U.S. Department of Commerce

Xerox Corporation's Business Products and Systems

For its first 15 years, Xerox was without equal, best in an industry whose products were synonymous with its name. But challenges did come in the mid-1970s from foreign and U.S. competitors who surpassed Xerox reprographic products in both cost and quality.

Not even second best in some product categories, Xerox launched an ambitious quality improvement program in 1984 to arrest its decline in the world market it had created.

Today, the company can once again claim the title as the industry's best in nearly all copier-product markets. As a result, Xerox has not only halted loss of world market share, but also reversed it.

Xerox Business Products and Systems (BP&S), headquartered in Stamford, Connecticut, attributes the turnaround to its strategy of Leadership Through Quality. The company defines quality through the eyes of the customer. Perhaps more so than any other company— inside and outside the copier industry—Xerox BP&S knows what customers want in products and services.

Analyses of a wide variety of data, gathered with exhaustive collection efforts that include monthly surveys of 55,000 Xerox equipment owners, enable the company to identify customer requirements. The company uses this information to develop concrete business plans with measurable targets for achieving quality improvements necessary to meet customer needs.

Xerox at a Glance

One of two Xerox Corporation businesses, Business Products and Systems employs 50,200 people at 83 U.S. locations. BP&S makes more than 250 types of document-processing equipment, generating more than $6 billion in 1988 U.S. sales, or 54 percent of the company's domestic revenues. Copiers and other duplicating equipment account for nearly 70 percent of BP&S revenues. The remainder is divided among sales of electronic printers and typing equipment, networks, workstations, and software products.

Xerox introduced the world's first plain-paper copier in 1959 and to this day is the largest provider of copiers and electronic printers. Nearly 30 percent of the more than 4 million copiers installed in the United States are Xerox machines.

Leadership Through Quality

Directed by CEO David T. Kearns and his senior management team, the Leadership Through Quality thrust has made quality improvement and, ultimately, customer satisfaction the job of every employee. All have received at least 28 hours of training in problem-solving and quality improvement techniques. The company has invested more than four million labor hours and $125 million in educating employees about quality principles.

Workers are vested with authority for day-to-day work decisions, and they are expected to take the initiative in identifying and correcting problems that affect the quality of products or services. Both salaried and hourly personnel have embraced these added responsibilities. For example, the company's 1989 labor contract with the Amalgamated Clothing and Textile Workers Union pledges employee support for "continuous quality improvement while reducing quality costs through teamwork and the tools and processes of Leadership Through Quality." This partnership with the union is considered a model by other corporations.

The phrase "Team Xerox" is not an empty slogan. It accurately reflects the firm's approach to tackling quality issues. Xerox BP&S estimates that 75 percent of its workers are members of at least one of more than 7,000 quality improvement teams. In 1988, teams in manufacturing and development were credited with saving $116 million by reducing scrap, tightening production schedules, and devising other efficiency and quality-enhancing measures.

Teamwork also characterizes the company's relationship with many of its 480 suppliers. Suppliers are "process qualified" through a step-by-step procedure to analyze and quantify suppliers' production and control processes. Suppliers receive training and follow up in such areas as statistical process control and total quality techniques; firms credit Xerox with improving their products and operations. For BP&S, increasing reliance on qualified suppliers over the last five years has reduced the number of defective parts reaching the production line by 73 percent.

Planning new products and services is based on detailed analyses of data organized in 375 information management systems, including 175 specific to planning, managing, and evaluating quality improvement. Much of this wealth of data has been amassed through an extensive network of market surveillance and customer feedback, all designed to support systematic evaluation of customer requirements. Over half of the company's marketing research is allocated for this purpose, and each year its Customer Service Measurement System tracks the behavior and preferences of about 200,000 owners of Xerox equipment.

Benchmarking System

In its quest to elevate its products and services to world-class status, Xerox BP&S devised a benchmarking system that has become a model. The company measures its performance in about 240 key areas of product, service, and business performance. Derived from international studies, the ultimate target in each area is the level of performance achieved by the world leader, regardless of industry. The BP&S benchmark for meeting daily production schedules, for example, is the near-perfect record achieved by Cummins Engine Company. Similarly, Xerox studied L.L. Bean for improvements in distribution and American Express for expertise in billing.

Returns to the company's strategy for continuous quality improvement have materialized quickly. Gains in quality over the last five years include a 78-percent decrease in the number of defects per 100 machines; greatly increased product reliability, as measured by a 40-percent decrease in unscheduled maintenance; increasing copy quality, which strengthened the company's position as world leader; a 27-percent drop (nearly two hours) in service response time; and significant reductions in labor and material overhead. These improvements have enabled Xerox BP&S to take additional steps to distinguish itself from the competition; for instance, it was the first in the industry to offer a three-year product warranty.

Customers have noticed the improvements. In 1984, competitors' machines ranked higher in customer satisfaction in all six product categories, according to Xerox surveys. Today, Xerox copiers top five of the six categories in Xerox surveys and rank similarly in industry surveys. Coincidentally, the increase in customer satisfaction parallels the company's gain in world market share over the same span.

The thrust of Leadership Through Quality is ongoing with Xerox BP&S. The process of continual quality improvement, directed toward greater customer satisfaction and enhanced business performance, has currently targeted a 50-percent reduction in unit manufacturing cost and a fourfold improvement in reliability by 1993. Such goals illustrate the commitment contained in the Xerox Quality Policy, which states that "quality is the basic business principle at Xerox."

Source: U.S. Department of Commerce

ACKNOWLEDGMENTS

THE CUTTING edge of the movement to restore quality and service in American business is an exciting place to be. Those who are at the forefront, who provide the insights, and who dare to challenge conventional ways are exceptional persons. I thank these people for allowing me to be privy to their knowledge and creative ideas.

High on the list of leaders in the quality and service renaissance are the Nordstroms of Seattle, Washington where I live. The Nordstrom family, in its department store operations, has created a model of customer service to which many aspire but few attain. Beyond running a successful business, the Nordstroms are civic leaders who bring their high values to their industry and to the Seattle community.

Special recognition is also due Burt Staniar, chairman of Westinghouse Broadcasting. Mr. Staniar is a leader in understanding both the practical and ethical values of quality and customer service. An arm of his company, the Commercial Nuclear Fuel Division of Westinghouse Electric, was one of only three companies that won the first annual Malcolm Baldrige National Quality Award in 1988. From a personal standpoint, I owe thanks to Mr. Staniar for having faith in me and giving me the opportunity and encouragement to explore, learn, and put into practice the concepts of customer retention when I was associated with Westinghouse cable television operations.

Other leaders to whom I owe appreciation for their ideas and research input to this book include Donald Petersen, chairman and CEO of the Ford Motor Company; Leon Gorman, president of L. L. Bean; Judith Rogala, senior vice president at Federal Express; Luke Helms, president of Seafirst Bank; Jon M. Christoffersen, John D. Mangels, chairman, Security Pacific Bank of Washington; and Michael Sims, senior vice president of Warner Amex.

My thanks also go to Curt Reimann, the always good-natured, unflappable gentleman who is the guiding hand for the Malcolm Baldrige National Quality Award at the Department of Commerce's National Institute of Standards and Technology.

Additional sources of information and valuable ideas include the professional staffs at the Technical Assistance Research Programs Institute (TARP) and the American Society of Quality Control (ASQC).

Deep personal thanks go to my colleague and close friend, Kathie Lehner, who acted as a sounding-board, critic, and brainstorming partner in thinking through this book, and Jennifer Fenswick, whose highly able, tireless, and creative support helps keep our own "shop" running. To Melody Kegley for being so understanding.

I also want to acknowledge the professional advice and guidance given by my editor, Virginia Smith of Harper Business, a division of Harper & Row. And finally, I extend my sincere appreciation to Marjorie Richman, of Cambridge, Massachusetts, who first recognized the possibilities of this book; Ron Bingaman, of the Isle of Palms, South Carolina, whose ideas on quality helped shape the final manuscript; and Dave Jepsen and Cindy Dowdell, who both worked on the project with such proficiency and good humor.

LAURA A. LISWOOD

INTRODUCTION

POOR CUSTOMER service in America, much like the decline in the quality of American manufactured goods, is one of management's costliest problems. Yet service remains a seriously neglected part of most businesses.

Every executive knows the high cost of getting new customers, but fewer seem to realize the high cost of *losing* customers. This is partly because selling and marketing are the action-packed sides of the business, whereas customer service—the job of keeping customers once you've won them—is generally seen as a drab, tedious, "maintenance" job.

When asked how their customer service is, most managers today give answers that are either ambivalent or that smack of downright indifference. "It's not too bad," they'll say, or "It's better than most." "Sure, we lose some customers, but what are you going to do about it? They die, they move away, or somebody down the street gives them a better price."

It's like knocking and finding nobody's there. Customer service is not a pleasant subject to many of today's managers. Neither is it a pleasant subject to customers. When you ask customers about the quality of service they're getting, the cacophony of complaints can be almost deafening. Suddenly, everybody's got plenty to say on the subject because, after all, everybody is a consumer, and there are few consumers in the United States who don't have a list of horror stories to tell about shabby treatment at the hands of insensitive clerks, indifferent managers, or insensate computers. We're not referring to the occasional, isolated, even expectable instances of poor service. Human beings are imperfect, and we can't presume that our every venture into the marketplace will be a totally pleasing experience. Salespeople, bank tellers, airline ticket agents, and furnace repairmen have bad days from time to time. They may carry last night's domestic quarrel to work with them, they may be feeling under the weather, or they might be smarting from some mistreatment they've just suffered themselves at the hands of a rude customer or an abusive boss.

The critical issue is that customer service in the United States has plunged far below any realistic level of minor and random breakdowns. Poor service, in fact, has become almost endemic to American business. And at a time when two out of every three jobs are service-related, the problem can no longer be ignored or treated as a peripheral concern.

There have always been poorly run companies, of course, and many of them have somehow found a way to survive longer than they deserved—often because they were "the only game in town" and sometimes because they played with stacked decks. But the rules and conditions are rapidly changing, and the number and caliber of players are rising almost exponentially. Few companies today enjoy for any length of time a monopoly or even a decided dominance in their markets. Competition in most lines of business is becoming crowded, sophisticated, and fierce. This is true both in domestic competition and in the struggle to cope with imports and the increasingly entangled webs of multinational market arrangements. For companies that don't learn how to keep customers once they've acquired them, the issue, quite simply, is survival. The proper treatment of customers—or what we refer to in business terminology as "service delivery"— is now a life-and-death management concern. But while a growing number of top executives with leading corporations are beginning to get this message, there remains a formidable lineup of myopic attitudes, outmoded management methods, and corporate structural impediments that make it difficult to craft workable strategies for retaining customers. Enlightened managers know what's needed, but there are many entrenched barriers standing in the way. Also, far too many managers remain *un*enlightened. They may suppose—even insist—that their companies are customer-oriented and that they do a good job of service delivery. They often proudly recite the clichés: "The customer is king!" "The customer always comes first." "The most important people in the world are our customers." But there's a big gap between this kind of superficial sloganeering and actually getting the job done. To hold on to customers in today's marketplace of intense and fast-paced competition, companies have to make a giant leap from *lip* service to *real* service.

Across-the-board improvements in customer service will not come easily or quickly in much of American business. Complacency and lack of understanding run too deep, and internal corporate power structures are heavily weighted in favor of traditional roles and functions that all but exclude good service management. Finance people historically have thought of finance as the backbone of the company; product people tend to think of the physical product or marketable service as the most important element; and legal departments are typically focused on their own set of specialized concerns, which in today's business environment increasingly center around mergers, acquisitions, and greenmail. It's as though most businesses are run purely for the sake of "doing business"—not for the purpose of satisfying customer needs and wants. Everybody may be tending the store, but few are tending the customer.

My idea for writing this book has evolved over the 12 years I've spent as a manager and consultant in service delivery and customer relations. From a professional standpoint, my job is to be critical and analytical about the state of customer service in America. But, like everyone else, I am also a consumer; and it certainly doesn't require a professional mind-set to become a disillusioned, frustrated, and ultimately irate consumer. All of us have become eminently qualified for that role in recent years.

I have worked in the lost-luggage department of a major airline on Christmas Eve and seen normally reasonable, good-tempered travelers go into screaming rages or break down and weep because their belongings were lost; and nobody knew—or *cared*—why or what to do about it.

I have spent part of my career in cable television, where, out of disgust and anger over poor service, otherwise honest customers felt justified in stealing cable services, rationalizing that the company owed it to them.

I have also watched in amazement while, on any given day, almost as many customers of the banking industry closed accounts as opened them.

But there *is* hope. And there *are* companies and institutions that are encouraging the kind of fundamental rethinking and positive steps needed to restore real service to our economy. We'll talk about some of these companies and institutions later in the book. Among them are such well-known names as the Ford Motor Company, L. L. Bean, Disney Productions, Corning Glass Works, Federal Express, and McDonald's.

It is also reassuring to know that our federal government is beginning to bring its considerable influence to bear on the problem of poor service and low product quality. The seeds of government concern were sown in the 1970s, when the United States began to lose so heavily in the international marketplace—when a "Made in the U.S.A." label became a mark of questionable quality, and the work ethic of our labor force became suspect. From those grim days through most of the 1980s, the tendency in Washington as well as in much of private industry was to defend our economy through anti-import legislation. But with or without such defensive measures, there is a growing realization that the only lasting solution is to restore excellence to America's goods and services.

One expression of this new attitude comes through the Malcolm Baldrige National Quality Improvement Act of 1987. Sponsored by the U.S. Department of Commerce and named for its late Secretary, Malcolm Baldrige, this congressionally authorized program provides for annual National Quality Awards to be presented by the President of the United States to domestic companies that demonstrate exceptional performance in product quality and service delivery. Some observers have called it "the Nobel Prize for business," and it's no secret that the Baldrige Award is patterned closely after Japan's Deming Award, which is taken very seriously by Japanese companies, media, and government leaders. Ironically, the Deming Award is named for an American—W. Edwards Deming— whose quality and productivity ideas were spurned by U.S. automakers before he took his know-how to Japan and helped create the immensely successful Japanese auto industry. The American Society for Quality Control and the American Productivity & Quality Center administer the judging for the Baldrige Award, and the standards are extremely demanding. No more than six awards may be granted per year, with a maximum of two awards in each of three business categories: manufacturing, service industry, and small business. To win, a company must excel at more than 275 explicit criteria in such areas as the leadership qualities of management, employee involvement, human resources, quality process controls, and customer satisfaction.

Underscoring the seriousness of the program is the fact that in its first year (1988) President Reagan conferred awards on only three companies instead of the six authorized by law. The winners were Motorola, the Commercial Nuclear Fuel Division of Westinghouse, and Globe Metallurgical (a small Ohio-based producer of specialty alloys). These three firms were singled out from a total of 63 entrants, only 13 of which made it to the final stage of intensive quality audits conducted on-site by teams of industrial, technological, and academic experts. It should be noted, too, that all three winners are manufacturers. Even though two were authorized, *no* awards were given to service or retailing industries.

Psychologists say that any one or a combination of three things is needed to overcome resistance to change: (1) a cataclysmic event, (2) a clear vision of where the change will lead, and (3) the experience of taking the first step in a new direction.

For many American businesses, the first condition—a cataclysmic event—is already a reality or is lurking just beneath the surface, like an incipient earthquake. It may be manifested as a plunge in market share, as unsustainable financial losses, or as a major threat from a new competitor. Whatever the case, the cataclysm will either force the company to change for the better or will drive it out of business.

The second condition for change—a clear vision of where you want to go—is one that tests the leadership qualities of any management group. In the context of this book, that vision is indelibly clear. American companies *must* set their sights on improving service delivery, product quality, and customer satisfaction.

As for the third conditon, taking those first steps can be scary, but you'll never get anywhere if you don't start. Some companies have already started, and we can learn from them. Senior executives of the Baldrige Award-winning companies and other quality-oriented firms say that building a total quality program means taking risks and that every company at first will have its cynics who predict failure. But there's more risk in *not* shaping up than there is in making the big changes and trying the new techniques that can improve quality. Now that the quality fervor has begun to catch on in American business, companies that don't take risks and silence the cynics will fall further and further behind.

There are longstanding barriers to quality and good customer service, and in this book we'll examine those that are most persistent and hard to overcome. We'll study distinct tactics and techniques for improving service delivery and raising customer satisfaction levels. We'll also talk about the nuts and bolts of service-delivery management and the ongoing commitment that it takes to sustain an effective program once you've got it in place. Along the way, we'll discuss the need to elevate service delivery to a management science status so that it can take its place among the traditional seats of corporate power and policymaking. To that end, we are proposing the development of a new type of corporate executive: the *Chief Service Officer*, or *CSO*. A job description for the CSO is included, along with an education/career-path profile denoting the qualifications that such a person should have. It is also time to employ a professional structure for setting standards and systematically evaluating quality and service performance throughout business and industry. In Chapter 5, I propose a formal program called Generally Accepted Service Principles (GASP ^{TM}) to monitor the delivery of service and customer satisfaction. Kenneth E. Leach, vice president for administration and chief quality officer at Globe Metalurgical, emphasizes that quality depends heavily upon consistency, and consistency cannot be maintained without continuous measurement against established standards and customer expectations.

A study published recently by *U.S. News & World Report* shows that *68 percent* of the customers who stop buying from a particular company do so because of employee indifference toward their needs and wants; only 14 percent stop buying because of product dissatisfaction. These figures are a damning commentary on the way the majority of American companies actually view their customers. And as American businesses continue to lose in both the domestic and foreign marketplaces, it's clear that massive improvement is desperately needed. John C. Marous, chairman of Westinghouse Electric, recently told a "Quest for Excellence" Conference in Washington, D.C. that "total quality is the absolute answer to *all* of our problems, professionally and personally, in this country."

There's no mystery or magic involved in achieving total quality: just clear-headed analysis, the courage to take risks and allocate money, a willingness to share responsibility and rewards with employees, and an intense commitment to the ideal of creating value and satisfaction for customers. Robert Galvin, chairman of Motorola, says the commitment has to be "deeply personal" and that real change won't take place until this personal feeling is transmitted throughout the ranks. And John Marous adds that "total quality is a cultural change which requires an *emotional* experience."

It's long past time that all of us got very emotional, indeed, about the sorry state of product quality and customer service in America.

1

NO SALE IS
EVER FINAL

STANLEY MARCUS, of the Neiman-Marcus department store organization, once said: "Why do you think you have so many department stores in a mall these days? It's because each of them does such a poor selling job that they survive just by taking up each other's unsatisfied customers."

What a terrible indictment of the American department store industry! But it isn't just department stores that are at issue. Everywhere you look, you find growing dissatisfaction among consumers and business buyers alike. So far, the quality-improvement crusade in American manufacturing has barely touched the retailing and service industries. Stanley Marcus pinpointed "poor selling," but that's not the problem. In most industries, we're *too* adept at pushing inferior goods and poorly performed services. What really counts is whether the customer feels good about the buying experience and remains happy after the sale. Are we delivering real satisfaction? Are we backing up the commitment that we make when we take a customer's money? Very few American companies can give

1

positive answers to those questions. Far too often, courteous and attentive treatment of the customer is viewed only as a selling tactic; the concern quickly dissipates with the close of the sale. "Customer satisfaction" frequently means little more than the wording used in advertising or on product or service warranties, as in "Satisfaction Guaranteed!" And commitment to the customer often turns out to be only an empty or fragile promise.

As we enter the 1990s, more top executives are recognizing the severity of this problem. People who less than a decade ago wouldn't have questioned America's performance and know-how in everything from street sweeping to moon landings are now openly critical of the appallingly low levels of product and service quality in the United States. Even the National Aeronautics and Space Administration (NASA) admits that, "until only recently, the worldwide superiority of the U.S. aerospace industry has been unassailable. However, U.S. aerospace industry leaders are now justifiably concerned that their economic future may be in jeopardy similar to the experience of other U.S. industries such as steel, auto, and electronics." In 1987, a Gallup survey of 615 American corporate leaders revealed that a majority believed the improvement of service and product quality is the most crucial challenge to our economy in the immediate future. As James R. Houghton, chairman of Corning Glass Works, put it: "Our business leaders are now more aware that attention to quality is the critical factor between success and failure."

It will take much more than the publication of a few surveys or the words of a few forward-thinking executives to reverse the suicide course that many American companies are following. True, no real improvements are possible unless the highest echelons of management understand the problem and make a commitment to solving it. However, higher product quality and good customer service depend on a commitment by *everyone* associated with the creation and delivery of that product or service. What is said in the executive suites and boardrooms has to be reflected in what is done out in the trenches, and the intervening territory can be full of obstacles.

Most large companies and even many smaller ones are encumbered by traditionally rigid organizational structures, narrowly defined functions and roles, deadening rules and procedures, and internal politics. At a meeting of more than 700 manufacturing executives in Dayton, Ohio in late 1988, Wickham Skinner, a Harvard Business School professor, cited corporate bureaucracy as a key reason for America's quality crisis. American companies, Skinner explained, are so highly departmentalized that different sectors of a company often work at cross-purposes. Each department has its own set of objectives, attitudes, and special interests, and when the self-interest of one department clashes with that of another, the usual result is mediocre performance all around.

Caught in such a maze of bureaucracy and internal game-playing, a company tends to lose sight of its main objective: satisfying its customers. Managers and workers alike are preoccupied with how to make it through the day within the system, and this mind-set diverts attention, time, energy, and skills away from the job of creating product value and customer satisfaction. Customers don't care how your day-at-the-office is going. They're not interested in what's happening inside the company, unless it involves something unethical or illegal. Customers really care about the utility and satisfaction that your product or service is supposed to give them.

Although a few perceptive business leaders may be getting the point about poor quality, many thousands of other owners, corporate executives, middle managers, and front-line personnel are continuing with business as usual. Even when faced with a customer drain, they typically blame almost anything but the real culprits: subpar products and bad service. The conventional wisdom says that customers come and customers go; that's merely one of the inevitabilities of being in business. It's easy to shrug your shoulders and fall back on the same alibis that just about everybody else uses: customers die, retire, get divorced, go bankrupt, move away, or no longer need a diaper service because the kid finally got potty-trained.

Fine. With most products or services, there are certain uncontrollable reasons why customers stop buying. But there are also *controllable* reasons, and too many people today don't know the difference between controllable and uncontrollable. Most companies don't know how, or don't take the trouble, to identify and track the reasons why their customers leave. Even those that do are inclined to write off many customer losses where opportunities for continuing business still exist. Just because customers move away doesn't mean they're completely or permanently beyond reach. Your firm might have a branch near a customer's new home; or, depending on your product or service, you might still be able to do business by mail or phone.

Even more damaging—and inexcusable—is the attitude that unhappy customers are merely complainers and are not worth the trouble it takes to satisfy them. There's no doubt that our society has its share of habitual squawkers, nitpickers, and outright thieves. But many businesses find it too easy to stick one of these labels on practically any customer who complains. Facing this attitude, every unhappy customer is more vulnerable to poor treatment without regard for the real merits of his or her problem.

Another pattern of thinking that contributes to poor service is the almost blind faith that many American business people have in *selling*. Whether it's an art, a science, or a little of both, selling is undeniably a high-skill task that is absolutely essential to bringing in business. But in America we've virtually made a fetish of the sales function, and when a disproportionate share of a company's efforts, resources, and rewards is focused on getting new customers, the job of *keeping* customers is typically short-changed.

Prospective and first-time customers are rarely treated badly, since the overriding objective is to make the sale. The new customer is enticed, seduced, persuaded—all of which add up to treating the customer with the utmost of care. New business can always be brought in the front door by good selling, but you have a revolving door if the service is bad. In they come, with great expectations; out they go, with disappointment and resentment. That's why no sale is ever final. Once the sales and marketing people have won a new customer, it's up to everybody to see that this customer remains sold.

The sales or overall marketing function should be viewed as a two-phased job: *getting* customers and *keeping* customers. The first phase rarely suffers from lack of attention or inadequate resources. Advertising, promotion, and sales budgets usually command enormous shares of a company's total operating budget. But "retention marketing"—the role of keeping those hard-won customers—has no budget at all. With a few exceptions, it is not even legitimized as a distinct part of doing business. Traditionally, it has existed only in fragments such as customer-complaint departments, returned-goods policies, guarantees and warranties, and an annual Christmas-card mailing. Not many companies pursue an organized, coherent strategy of retention marketing aimed at keeping customers happy or salvaging relations with unhappy customers. Most find it easier, instead, to go on competing for new customers—to keep that revolving door spinning fast enough to avoid a net loss of business.

Research shows that, depending upon the industry involved, it costs anywhere from five to seven times as much to get a new customer as it does to keep an existing one. Most companies have little trouble justifying the high costs of acquiring new customers, as long as those new customers represent a net increase in business. But what if the newcomers are merely replacements for old customers who have gone away mad? Every time you have to replace a lost customer, you must make another new investment to fill the *same* customer slot. And if that first customer did substantial business with you before leaving, you could end up spending ten to fourteen times as much replacing that customer as it would have taken to keep him or her happy.

80/20

This excess cost is compounded when we consider the "80/20" rule, which says that for many businesses 20 percent of the customers account for 80 percent of the sales volume. (Example: In banking, 15 to 20 percent of the clientele are typically responsible for 70 to 90 percent of the deposit and loan activity.) Clearly, the disappearance of any one customer from the 20-percent segment can be a severe loss. And it can be even worse if you don't replace that missing customer with another one who qualifies for the 20-percent club. In fact, it would require *five* new low-activity customers to replace the one big one who got away.

Seen in this light, retention marketing assumes far more significance than the passive, defensive role to which it is relegated in most companies. That role is often filled largely by a customer-complaint department. A 1988 survey of *Fortune 500* executives by Organizational Dynamics, Inc. (ODI) showed that 85 percent of the responding companies routinely tracked customer complaints. But a good retention-marketing program neither begins nor ends there. According to Y. S. Chang, ODI senior quality counsel and director of Boston University's Asian Management Center, "There is a danger in focusing too exclusively on customer complaints that track only the damage that's already been done." Overreliance on such data, Chang explains, can leave management in a "strictly reactive mode."

Reactive Mode

Complaints = Opportunities = Last chance

Ironically, complainants are often valuable customers because they're giving the company a chance to make good before they take their business elsewhere. And if their complaints are handled to their satisfaction, 90 percent of them will stay. Most of us, as customers, are afflicted with the common human condition of inertia. We don't really want to move our checking account, change dry cleaners, take a chance on a different model car, or try the chairside manner of a different dentist. We prefer to stick with what's familiar, as long as we continue to get reasonable satisfaction from it. But there's a limit, and we *will* change when the satisfaction level drops too low or when we're offered a superior alternative. Thus, in a company that's truly service-oriented, any complaint is really an *opportunity*—an opportunity to correct a problem or do something better and a second chance to preserve a valuable customer relationship.

Not all dissatisfied customers, however, take the trouble or risk the aggravation of complaining. Sometimes they simply don't come back. This depends partly upon the type and value of the product or service they've bought. The Technical Assistance Research Programs Institute (TARP), a consulting firm based in Washington, D.C., has studied the frequency of complaints relative to the type and price range of the purchase. TARP found that, for big-ticket durable goods, 60 percent of unhappy customers will complain; for medium-ticket durable goods, 50 percent will complain; on big-ticket services, only 37 percent of dissatisfied customers complain: and on small-ticket services, 45 percent do. The message is that low quality and poor service have become so common that 40 to 60 percent of customers are simply resigned to the situation and make no effort to get what's due them.

Most people dislike contentiousness and haggling. They would rather be treated fairly the first time and not be put in the position of having to insist on their rights. But when they do fight back, they want results. Research by TARP shows the effects of poor complaint-handling. With minor complaints involving a $1 to $5 adjustment, 95 percent of customers will buy again from the same company if their complaints are resolved quickly. Only 46 percent will buy again if their complaints are not resolved. And just 37 percent of unhappy customers who do *not* complain will come back for another purchase. For major complaints involving adjustments of more than $100, approximately 82 percent of the people will buy again if their complaints are resolved quickly; only 19 percent if their complaints go unresolved; and a scant 9 percent if the unhappy customers choose not to complain.

Both TARP studies suggest that American buyers are confused, ambivalent, and frustrated. They find it increasingly hard to get what they want, and they lack assurance that their complaints will be heard. Part of the problem is that many companies promise the moon and deliver a paper facsimile. Another part is the sheer noise and clutter of today's marketing. We are constantly bombarded with selling appeals: TV commercials, billing inserts, junk mail, doorknob pouches, Sunday newspapers bloated with advertising, and canned telephone sales pitches disguised as research or prize giveaways. Even with the most ethical companies, product claims are often exaggerated, and selling appeals are often manipulative and intrusive. All of this clamor and deception are making customers more skeptical. What they see in the ads is frequently not what they get when they plunk their money down or sign their credit card slip. In short, business is pouring vast resources into customer seduction but is neglecting to deliver customer satisfaction and assurance. Small wonder, then, that customers come and go, and that many of them don't even bother to complain. If this is unfair to the customer, it is also—or should be—disquieting to business. No company can sustain indefinitely a continuous turnover of dissatisfied customers. Before anything can be done about it, however, companies have to learn how to measure their customer turnover and track the specific reasons for it.

One customer-turnover measure used in the cable television industry is called "churn." The churn rate is the ratio between new subscribers and lost subscribers in a year's time. For example, if 40,000 subscribers cancel and 50,000 new ones sign up, the churn would be 80 percent. Naturally, the lower this rate, the better. However, for certain nationwide cable services, such as HBO and Showtime, customer churn often exceeds 100 percent, which means that more people are cancelling than are signing up. Interestingly, this may not be so much a reflection of poor service as it is of overselling. In any case, a high churn rate is costly. Assume, for example, that a cable operator spends $2 million on marketing to get 50,000 new customers—a cost of $40 per customer. If during this same period 40,000 existing customers cancel their subscriptions, the company has a *net* gain of only 10,000 new subscribers. That means it really cost $200 per subscriber to add to the customer base.

In financial institutions, customer churn can be applied to any number of operations or transactions. The most telling churn rate (as in cable TV) compares the number of new accounts opened to the number closed. Of course, this rate can be affected by general economic conditions locally, regionally, or nationally. But after such trends are taken into account, it can also indicate how well or badly the institution is treating its customers. Banking industry statistics show that fewer than half of all customers leave a particular bank because they move out of its service area. The majority leave because they are dissatisfied with one or more *controllable* facets of the bank's customer offering such as fees, rates, other pocketbook values, and quality of service. What many bank executives fail to realize is that good service can often outweigh unfavorable money factors. Customers may know they can get a better interest rate, free checks, or lower service fees at a bank down the street, but they'd rather stay where they are if they are treated as valued customers.

As competition in almost every line of business continues to heat up, companies that hope to survive must pay more and more attention to how their customers behave. Although a customer may be an asset, he or she is not a "commodity" and cannot be handled as such. Today's customers have higher expectations and a stronger sense of entitlement. Government, social institutions, and businesses themselves have been telling us for years that we are *entitled* to certain things. We have rights, including "consumer rights." Ralph Nader built an entire career for himself and his coterie of consumer advocates by lobbying for consumer protection. But smart management doesn't stop at what Ralph Nader or the government says is minimal. Winning companies go far beyond what the law requires or what people have been taught to expect. Spencer Hutchens, Jr., senior vice president of Intertek Services, says that "The winning strategy is not simply

to satisfy your customers' basic requirements, but to go
beyond their expectations so they'll become loyal buyers
who keep coming back."

Many retailing analysts and consultants are warning us
that the United States today is "over-stored." By some
estimates, we have twice the retail and service establish-
ments needed to effectively serve our population. But the
concern is not merely for an overabundance of retail store
buildings or square footage of selling space. The broader
issue involves an excess of all types of players in the
merchandising and service arenas. New forms of retailing have added to the "store count" and the marketing
clutter. In recent years, we have seen rapid expansion
in mail-order marketing, catalogue stores, telemarketing,
phone soliciting, and computerized marketing services.
We have wholesale clubs, self-serve discount warehouses,
buying cooperatives, party selling, door-to-door hawking,
curbside services, and so on—including the old-fashioned
walk-in store that sits in one place long enough to get
an ad in the *Yellow Pages*. Fixed retailing sites are scat-
tered among traditional shopping centers, strip centers,
regional malls, mixed-use malls, neighborhood clusters,
and boutique shopping districts in renovated downtown
areas. The latest twist is the so-called "power center,"
which is supposed to fit conceptually somewhere between
a strip center and a regional mall. And at many street-
corners, highway crossroads, and freeway exits we find
the ubiquitous convenience store.

The net effect is that a visitor from another planet might
suspect we have more sellers than buyers, more stores
than homes, and more goods and services than we need or
even want. We also have specialists who create new needs
and wants to keep us on the buying treadmill. Clearly, the
advertising and promotion people are doing a stellar job.
So, too, are a number of other experts. Consultants, for
example, will tell you how to dress for success, how to
develop a "power image," how to behave at social functions, and how to make your leisure time more "produc-

tive." Others tell you how to enjoy sex, what to do when your kid comes home with a bloody nose, how to recycle your garbage, and how to have a "meaningful" life after 55. There's something for everybody: products and services catering to every conceivable whim. And new whims are being invented almost daily.

Sociologists and psychologists can ponder why we are turning to these external support systems to define ourselves. The practical reality for a business is that buyers are offered a seemingly endless variety of choices. Customers don't really have to put up with poor service or unmet expectations. They can take their buying dollars elsewhere, and elsewhere is often just around the corner or in the telephone directory. As bad as product quality and customer service have become in general, there are still many companies offering superior choices, and there are convenient ways for people to take advantage of those choices. Old transactional and delivery barriers are gone, supplanted by quick, easy, economical methods of shopping, paying, and taking delivery. Today, a customer at home in Walla Walla, Washington can pick up the phone and order a down-filled vest from a store in Maine that is open 24 hours a day every day of the year. A credit card number from a New York or San Francisco bank pays for the purchase, and an express package service will deliver the vest as a gift to the buyer's friend in Atlanta or Phoenix within one or two days. The point is that many buying and selling channels no longer follow traditional patterns. They criss-cross, overlap, and take each other's place; and, of course, there are totally new channels. Whatever the realignments may be, the most important thing to the customer is the service experience. Did the customer get prompt, friendly, helpful treatment and a sincere thank-you when making the phone-call? When the vest arrived at its destination, was it the right size, color, and style? Did it get there in one or two days, as promised? And when the customer's credit card statement came a month later, was the purchase billed correctly?

Today's customers put a high premium on reliability, assurance, responsiveness, friendliness, clear communication, and security in the buying experience. Even if the price is right and the product or marketed service is of the highest quality, the failure to meet any one of these expectations can leave the customer dissatisfied with the entire transaction. Studies by the Forum Corporation—a training, consulting, and research firm—show that customers are *five* times more likely to switch vendors because of perceived service problems than for price or product-quality concerns.

It is important to remember, too, that people's perceptions and expectations are constantly changing. As customers move from one buying experience to another, they are exposed to different types and levels of service, and their future expectations will typically be based upon the *best* experience they've had in the past. This means the best in any circumstance, regardless of the type of merchandise or service involved. It's not simply a matter of comparing one bank to another bank or one department store to another department store. For example, anyone who's been to Disneyworld knows what cleanliness and friendliness mean, and they're apt to wonder: "Why can't *every* business be run this way?" Likewise, anyone who has used Federal Express knows the meaning of reliability, and people who patronize McDonald's know what consistency is all about. There is no double standard. People are less inclined to be tolerant about a 30-minute wait in a bank line once they have seen Disneyworld handle massive crowds quickly, efficiently, and with an air of good cheer.

Nor is there a double standard where technology is concerned. Most people applaud the benefits that advanced technology brings to everyday life. Computers, fiber optics, robotics, and other high-tech developments have made many routine tasks easier, faster, and more economical—not just in the workplace but in the marketplace as well. Up to one-third of a bank's customers never walk inside the bank, choosing instead to use drive-up windows, automated teller machines, or banking by mail, phone, or computer. All this is fine as long as the machines and software systems work properly and human error doesn't cause a snafu. But when a breakdown does occur in a technical system, customers can quickly lose their tolerance and their appreciation for the benefits of technology. There are few things in modern American life that can be more frustrating than being caught up in a computer twilight zone where common sense doesn't seem to apply. Being billed for something you didn't buy, getting past-due notices on a bill you paid two months ago, receiving the wrong (or defective) merchandise from a telemarketing or mail-order company, or having the bank teller machine print out "insufficient funds" when you know darn well you've got thousands of dollars sloshing around in there somewhere are the kinds of experiences that breed mistrust and resentment in even the most good-natured of customers. So, too, are the "lost" hotel reservations when you try to check in late at night after your airline flight arrived an hour behind schedule.

No matter how technologically advanced we get, customer-service standards must still be written in human terms and be bound by human conditions. Computers may "talk" to each other, and merchandise shipments may be routed electronically, but always at the paying end of a transaction is a *person* who is trying to get, with a minimum of pain, what's been promised to him or her. Indeed, the more computerized and mechanized our marketplace becomes, the more we need to immunize customers against system breakdowns. Customers and sellers used to be in close touch; now the touching is more and more between customers and machines. People punch buttons, pull levers, and dial dials to get what they want. But when the machine doesn't do its job right, a human being ought to be there, ready to ensure that the customer is ultimately satisfied. Even when everything works to technical perfection, the impersonality of automated transactions creates an emotional void for many customers. The more people have to use machines for the routine parts of a transaction, the more they want something to fill that void. They want a more congenial environment, a sense that the company really respects and values them as customers, and assurance that if things don't go as programmed, somebody in that company will fix it for them promptly, cheerfully, and accurately.

In effect, increasing automation has given business a mandate to treat customers better. Since automation is supposed to help companies operate more efficiently and profitably, some of the gains ought to be passed along to customers, not merely in the form of lower prices but in better service and even new services that will help people feel that *they*—not the machines—are ultimately in control of their lives.

Retention Marketing: The Second Half of the Sale

Acquisition marketing, or making the initial sale, is the way new customers are brought to a company. Retention marketing, or providing outstanding service, is the way a company keeps those customers coming back.

In the past, acquisition and retention marketing went hand in hand. Selling and service were part of the same ongoing company-customer relationship. By doing business with an establishment, a customer was automatically entitled to certain service rights: the rights to fair, courteous, and friendly treatment and the assurance that the proprietor would make good on anything that went wrong. However, as we matured into a more mobile, industrialized, technocratic society, a distinction arose between selling and everything that came after the sale. Selling became so specialized that it got to be called "marketing," and the job of attracting attention to a company or product evolved into "advertising and promotion." With the relentless growth in population, consumer demand, and purchasing power, everybody got so busy selling, promoting, and keeping score that owners and managers began to neglect the second half of the sale: the half where customers were supposed to be happy about turning over their money. We relegated the second half of the sale to "customer complaint departments," "service departments," and "warranty departments." That situation might have turned out fine, except that the job of providing service didn't furnish the glamor, excitement, and income associated with marketing and promotion. Among the biggest business stars, next to the financial managers, were the super-salespeople and advertising geniuses. A whole new mentality got wired into business thinking. A company's success was measured almost solely in terms of sales and revenue growth, and annual reports and internal documents reflected this one dimensional perspective. Management careers rested on the growth curves for unit sales, hotel occupancy rates, airline seats sold, or number of meals served.

This mentality has been reflected for years in the formal structures, hierarchies, and budgeting philosophies of companies. Acquisition marketing and promotion continue to dominate, while customer-service activities are typically underbudgeted, understaffed, viewed strictly as cost centers, and assigned to the periphery of a company's competitive strategy. But it's long past time for a shakeup. As demonstrated by such truly service-oriented companies as Federal Express and Disney Productions, customer service is far more than a maintenance function, and a retention-marketing program can be as important a part of a firm's strategic mix as selling, advertising, and promotion.

Every point where the customer comes into contact with the company—whether in person, by phone, or by mail—is a point of service delivery. It's a moment when the customer gains one more impression and forms one more judgment about the company or its product. It is, indeed, a moment of truth.

Jan Carlzon, president and CEO of the Scandinavian Airlines System (SAS), describes such moments in his book by the same name: *Moments of Truth* (Ballinger, 1987). Carlzon notes that in 1986, each of his company's 10 million customers came into contact with approximately five SAS employees, with each contact lasting an average of 15 seconds. "Thus," he wrote, "SAS is 'created' 50 million times a year, 15 seconds at a time. These 50 million 'moments of truth' are the moments that ultimately determine whether SAS will succeed or fail as a company. They are the moments when we must prove to our customers that SAS is their best alternative."

Each moment of truth, then, is actually a challenge to the company to make good on whatever it has led customers to expect. It's easy enough to make glowing promises, which most companies do; but there is often a wide gap between promise and reality. Consider these examples:

> *The Promise*: "Our department store is full-service."
> *The Reality*: Gift-wrap is in the basement, and it costs extra.
> *The Promise*: "Our clerks are trained to serve your needs."
> *The Reality*: The clerk has no authority to make a decision and tells the customer to come back when a supervisor is available.

Every time it fails to live up to a promise, a company has failed a test of truth and has lost a piece of its credibility. For many customers, one such disappointment is all it takes to send them elsewhere. Others may be tolerant enough to endure more than one broken promise, but eventually we all walk away from situations where we feel we're being taken for granted—or worse yet, simply *taken*.

Retention marketing must be concerned with *every* situation in which a customer might interact with the company. Advertising or public relations may create a highly favorable product or company image, and a firm might spend heavily on architecture, store layout, and decor. But it's the hundreds of smaller, less glamorous things that ultimately make the difference. It's the way a company's phones are answered, the appearance and behavior of *all* company personnel, the accuracy and clarity of billings, the promptness and reliability of handling complaints, and many other routine practices, as well as physical features, that determine a company's customer-friendliness. In short, it's a matter of details, details, and then more details. That's why it's so hard for many companies to go beyond the rhetoric of marketing and promotion to the actual delivery of good service. Consistent attention to detail isn't easy. As Walt Disney once said: "There is no magic to magic. It's in the details." But many people in business are always looking for a magical formula or sleight-of-hand technique that will give only the illusion of good service. What they're forgetting is another truism attributed to Abraham Lincoln: "You may fool all the people some of the time; you can even fool some of the people all the time; but you can't fool all of the people all the time." If that was true in Lincoln's era, it's no less true today. Customers will not be gulled or lulled forever. To earn and keep people's trust and loyalty, companies must rely less on banging their tambourines and concentrate more on listening for sounds of disbelief and discontent from their audience.

This means redefining the role of marketing, rearranging priorities, reallocating money, and learning better how to use the tools of retention marketing. The tools are already there in most cases, and many of them are already being used effectively in acquisition marketing. For example, sales and promotion personnel understand customer behavior. They know how to appeal to buyers' instincts. What better place to look, then, than to sales and promotion for an understanding of what makes customers happy? Yet we want to enlarge the dimension of this understanding. We need to know not merely what makes people buy in the first place but what makes them want to keep on buying the same product or patronizing the same company. Salespeople and advertising/promotion specialists can be rich sources of retention-marketing ideas if management can direct some of its know-how and enthusiasm in that direction.

Feedback from customers occurs constantly and naturally in the regular course of business, and a lot can be learned by purposefully listening and watching for a few telltale signs or by tracking and recording certain normal day-to-day activities. This, however, requires a commitment from management—a commitment and a willingness to play an active part. In too many companies, managers at upper and middle levels (or owners, in the case of proprietorships) lack the motivation or consider it inappropriate to get out in "the shop" and breathe the same air that customers and employees breathe. Their time and energies are consumed by meetings, reports, financial matters, and the like, while tiers of underlings shield them both from customers and from the employees who have daily contact with customers. The feedback that management gets from the front lines is usually filtered through several layers of employees who often see their jobs as being just that: "filters." The prevailing idea in many companies is that the boss doesn't want to be bothered by such mundane matters as service breakdowns or unhappily churning customers.

Feedback will come whether a company asks for it or not, and personnel at all levels should be trained and encouraged to recognize whatever feedback customers are offering either voluntarily or subconsciously. Many companies make overt efforts to stimulate feedback from their customers. But these efforts are often unimaginative and, worse, unconvincing to the customer. For example, "customer comment" cards are frequently small, drab, and cheaply printed. Lines are set too close together for people to conveniently write in their answers; the questions themselves are sometimes confusing; and the system for collecting the cards may leave the customer wondering if their real destination isn't simply the cleaning crew's trash cart. Here again, attention to detail is supremely important. Even awkward language or typographical errors on a comment card can be damaging.

The message delivered by offhanded or inept customer survey efforts is that the company doesn't *really* care what its customers think. It hasn't spent any serious time, money, or creative thought on the situation but is merely going through the motions and making an appearance of caring. Better to have no comment card at all than to have the customer think it's only a pretense. On the other hand, an honestly conceived, creatively designed, and carefully planned customer-feedback program can produce a treasure of information and, at the same time, serve as an ancillary public relations tool for heightening customer interest and confidence in the company.

If customer feedback is important, so too is feedback from employees—both from those on the front lines and those in the back rooms. Ordinarily, front-line employees are providers of service themselves and have frequent direct contact with customers. Backroom employees, while not typically exposed to customers, nonetheless can offer ideas on behind-the-scenes activities and procedures that affect customer service or product quality.

To get good feedback from employees, management must first *ask for it*. Most employees today see their jobs in a single, narrow dimension. They have grown up and lived their whole lives in a mass-production, mass-consumption atmosphere. That's true not just in factories but in most lines of retailing and services as well. For many years, our economy has been geared to job specialization. Many people spend entire careers or long segments of their working lives performing a single function day after day, isolated and insulated from the end product and its actual customer utility or satisfaction. Ordinarily, the people closest to the "end" in this sense are the salespeople or direct-service providers, who are in on the actual customer-product exchange. But even they have specialized jobs: closing the sale, writing the order, accepting the bank deposit, or unclogging the harried householder's kitchen sink. Their mental focus typically is on getting that one job done, and anything beyond that is usually considered to be "somebody else's problem." Yet these people are ideally placed to channel customer information back to management, and companies

are wasting a valuable resource if they fail to ask, motivate, and train their frontline personnel to take an active
part in gathering customer-satisfaction intelligence.

The ultimate payout for firms that do enlist both their
frontline and backroom employees in this function will
be not only better customer service but also a generally
more productive and loyal workforce. Most employees
take greater pride in their jobs and have greater respect
for their companies if they're convinced that management is honestly committed to serving the customers; and
most will respond when asked to enlarge their own contribution because it shows that the company also takes
them more seriously. Conversely, a company that is indifferent about customer satisfaction is usually pegged as
also being indifferent about its employees—and employees will sense this and resent it. At best, good employees will sooner or later tire of a job in which they are
constantly exposed to frustrated, irate customers and are
always being forced to wiggle out of indefensible situations.

Likewise, many backroom or plant employees will
become jaded about their jobs if they feel that management doesn't really care about product or service quality.
Whether it's in a clothing store alterations department, a
television repair shop, or an automobile assembly plant,
workers generally produce results no higher than the level
of management's expectations, and they will offer suggestions for improvement only if they know that somebody
in authority will honestly listen to them and appreciate
their concern. Forum Corporation research shows that the
number-one reason for employee turnover in the United
States is that workers believe their companies don't do a
good job or don't care about doing a good job of serving
customers. The second reason is that employees don't feel
their supervisors are letting them help create new ideas
for higher quality and better service.

A number of large companies, especially in manufacturing, now rely heavily on formal employee-feedback
programs to support their quality-improvement efforts,

and these programs typically reach throughout the work-force, including hourly as well as salaried personnel and line workers as well as supervisors. The first three Baldrige National Quality Award winners credit much of their recent success to innovative ideas from employees. Equally valuable to them are the higher morale, better spirit of cooperation, and greater personal pride in work that occur when management truly takes employees into its confidence and treats them as important contributors.

Motorola has its Participative Management Program (PMP), which brings together teams of employees who work in the same area or take part in specific quality-improvement projects. The Westinghouse Nuclear Fuels Division has some 1,500 employees in 175 quality-improvement teams. Globe Metallurgical, with only two plants and just 230 employees, has less of an internal communications challenge than the bigger companies, but Globe nonetheless has a formal employee-involvement system built around its Quality-Efficiency-Cost (QEC) program. The management-level QEC Committee meets daily at each plant, and hourly workers are organized into Quality Circles that meet weekly.

Other successful companies that are leaders in employee involvement include American Airlines, AT&T, Chrysler, General Motors, and Ford.

American Airlines, with one of the highest customer-service ratings in its industry, launched its Quality of Work Life Program in 1983 to create what chairman Robert L. Crandall described as "an environment based on trust and mutual respect." The airline today involves all of its employees, from baggage handlers and ticket agents to flight crews and senior managers, in a continuous quality-improvement effort.

At the AT&T Network Systems operation in Atlanta, quality teams are made up of hourly employees, managers, quality engineers, maintenance people, and union representatives. One AT&T executive has said that "The people who work in Atlanta run the plant as though it were their own business."

Chrysler is enlisting all of its employees in a concentrated effort to upgrade product quality. Chairman Lee Iacocca says he wants workers to feel that when they come to work they know they're contributing something "so that they can't wait to come back tomorrow."

General Motors and the United Auto Workers now collaborate in a UAW/GM Quality Network that involves every employee in looking for better ways to deal with people, material, equipment, work environment, methods, systems, and customer satisfaction. As described by Donald Ephlin, UAW vice president, the Quality Network means that "engineers will be talking to manufacturing folks, designers will be talking to engineers, dealers will be involved, workers will have input, and we will all be listening to the voice of the customer."

The Ford Motor Company's recent turnaround is a well-publicized example of how employee involvement can be crucial to a company's survival. In the early 1980s, Ford was nearly bankrupt from three straight years of huge financial losses. Product quality had dropped sharply, and the problem was blamed largely on Ford's hourly workers—a rap that was borne by GM and Chrysler workers too, under the assumption that America's industrial work ethic was disintegrating. A new management team had taken over at Ford after Henry Ford II retired in 1979, and this new leadership, under then-chairman Philip Caldwell, brought a different perspective to the company's problems. Breaking from Detroit's tradition of heavy-handed management and cold-war labor relations, Ford's leaders went to the hourly workers and asked their opinions on how to build better cars and improve productivity. Corporate executives, designers, engineers, and other salaried specialists went into the factories and talked with thousands of line workers and unit supervisors, openly urging them to give constructive criticism. With UAW cooperation, Ford set up an Employee Involvement (EI) program to furnish a permanent structure for employee participation at all levels. The operational results were an outpouring of innovative ideas, a rising of morale, and lessening of labor tension. By 1986, Ford was winning America's highest automotive quality awards, and in 1987 and 1988 the company set records for profitability in the auto industry while paying record-breaking bonuses to employees at all levels. Other factors contributed to this remarkable turnaround, but none of it would have happened without a successful employee involvement program. As Philip Caldwell put it: "Most employees truly *want* to do the right thing if you're honest and candid with them and if you treat them as adults and peers."

Ford and other innovative companies are not only winning new customers but also keeping them. And they're doing so both through a customer focus and by rallying *all* of their resources, from the CEO to the hourly employee. Whether it's in a manufacturing or airline company, bank, or department store, the job of keeping customers transcends hierarchies, crosses departmental boundaries, and requires communication and cooperation among people who historically have seen their jobs as specialized and insular. Corning chairman James R. Houghton says that a total quality program requires vision and leadership, but he adds that leaders are not just the CEOs. "You need people who lead at all levels, whether it's the head of the whole corporation or heads of individual work units," he explains. And while Houghton believes that quality leadership requires personal commitment and inspiration from the top, he also emphasizes that leaders must empower others in the organization to use their ideas and make decisions. Putting this philosophy into practice, Corning has created more than 1,500 problem-solving teams throughout the company. This is what participative management and employee involvement are all about.

Different companies have their own historical circumstances and will find their own unique mix of strategies and tactics for keeping customers. At the most basic level, however, a company must first commit to the need for retention marketing. It must understand that there's more profit in long-term customer relationships than in continuous turnover, or customer churn. Until a firm demonstrates that long-term relationships are important to it, customers have no reason to show loyalty. They may continue to buy for a while because of low price, brand familiarity, or just plain inertia. But the competition can lower its prices, bring out a superior new product, offer premiums and special incentives, or give better service. That's when we hear about customers being "fickle." Yet it's not the customer's responsibility to show appreciation or even to complain.

Consider the following scenario. A bank has been losing customers and has hired a consultant to find out why. The consultant says, "Let's have some focus groups and ask a few of your remaining customers what's wrong." So a focus group is scheduled—hopefully at a time and place convenient for the customers—and the first customer to speak out says, "I've been doing business with this bank for 20 years and not once have they ever thanked me. The only thing I ever get is a calendar with bird pictures on it. As a matter of fact, every time I try to cash a check, they still ask me for identification."

Is this a far-fetched scenario? Not at all. And it's just as valid for an airline, car dealership, restaurant, or insurance agency as it is for a bank. For all the push-button technology and mobility that shape our lives today, people still want to be treated *as people*. Consumers know that their names, addresses, social security numbers, and a lot of other personal data are tumbling around in dozens, if not hundreds, of computer systems; and they recognize it when they receive a piece of computer-generated mail (including a bird calendar). This makes it even more important that companies do as much as they can to make their customers feel special. It clearly isn't feasible for every single company-customer interaction to be deeply personalized, but a company *can* build and maintain a reputation for being customer-friendly and for being both capable of and willing to deal with unique customer needs as they come up.

It's hard to understand why management at some companies persists in ignoring or misreading the real needs of large segments of customers. Maybe it's as simple as the attitude displayed by a certain airline operations manager who said that *his* airplanes "could run on time if it just weren't for the passengers."

Yes, indeed. If it just weren't for the customers, life at the shop or plant might be ever so easy. But not likely very profitable.

2

MAJOR BARRIERS

IT'S SELF-DEFEATING for anyone in business to see his or her customers as the main barriers to good service. That isn't to say there aren't some customers who insist on the impossible or the unreasonable—people who won't be satisfied no matter how hard you try. But those exceptions don't justify the negative attitude of the airline operations manager who blames the passengers for his own service failure.

There are real barriers that any company must recognize and overcome in order to improve service. Many of them may be unique to specific industries, companies, products, market segments, or even locales. But there are some that we can think of as universal because they exist in one form or another for almost any type of business. In this chapter, we'll examine some of the most common of these barriers.

Barrier 1: The Differences in People

Many managers seem to forget one of the most basic facts of life: *no two people are alike*. True, we hear occasional lip service paid to this fact, but in practice it's easier to typecast individuals and to think in terms of group behavior. To a great extent, this is necessary in order to make an organization cohesive and manageable. But problems arise when managers begin to take people's behavior for granted or become desensitized to the individual qualities of employees and co-managers. This tendency is especially prevalent in manufacturing, where the assembly lines are like treadmills and line workers perform largely routine functions. It's hard for manufacturing executives and supervisors to interact with their people under these circumstances. However, managing the human element is no less a challenge in the distribution and service industries. With service delivery, each of the hundreds or thousands of people in a given company or service-delivery system functions more freely, responding to continuously changing situations and making moment-to-moment decisions. Because of their varying levels of skills, education, experience, interests, perceptions, values, and prejudices, all members are truly individuals. And in customer-contact or service-delivery jobs, the interplay of all these personal traits can have an immediate and direct impact on the outcome of any transaction or service function. Machines are incapable of making subjective judgments. Humans, however, decide when and how they will perform, depending upon how they feel. Thus, the human variables in service delivery are far greater than they are in the manufacturing of a product.

It is not that workers so often *try* to be difficult. Ordinarily, it's just the opposite. Most people will work hard to fit in and do what's asked or required. But how much control does a manager really have over the telephone representative who is going through a divorce? Or

the sales clerk whose baby is sick? Or the keypunch operator with money worries? All of these people are more
likely to make errors or react negatively to the customer
because of what's going on in their personal lives. In
addition, job-related apathy and boredom—two distinctly
human traits—can make normally sensitive, bright, and
caring people become indolent, cold, or downright rude.

Given such vagaries of human behavior, there are
no simple solutions or ten-easy-step formulas for dealing with people-related service-delivery problems. Every
clerk, teller, repair specialist, and telephone representative has to be trained, motivated, monitored, evaluated, and then periodically, if not continuously, *re*trained.

At Disneyland, management has applied some of its
famous creative talents to this human element of service
delivery and has chosen a special use of language, or terminology, to help employees feel good about themselves
while fitting into a team effort.

For example, anyone who deals with the public at Disneyland works "on stage," while all behind-the-scenes
areas such as back-up facilities, cafeterias, and maintenance are called "backstage."

The people who work at Disneyland are called "cast
members," not employees, and they are cast for specific
"roles" (or clear job responsibilities) in the Disneyland
"show." Furthermore, these cast members wear "cos-
tumes," not uniforms.

Most importantly, the people who come through the
gates are called "guests," not customers. If people were
known as customers, Disney management feels they
would be viewed as part of a faceless crowd of sales
prospects; but if they are "guests," they merit special, hos-
pitable treatment as individuals.

Some may consider this hokey or juvenile, but it works
for Disneyland. It offers employees a way to think of service as something beyond the role in which it is often seen:
as menial, low-skill work with a never-ending stream of
demanding customers.

*Employee
Apathy*

Consistency

Disney management also knows how to dispel or pre-vent employee apathy. The greatest threat to maintaining a positive environment for guests at Disneyland is not out-and-out rudeness but indifference. Someone may work in a position for a long while and never become rude, but their enthusiasm and desire to serve may weaken as time goes on. The lack of eye contact and the "It's-not-my-job" syndrome are some of the signs that apathy is setting in.

Customers want, among other service expectations, *consistency*. It is what makes people want the same waiter or bank teller. They enjoy the personal recognition and they also value the predictability of treatment that comes from the familiar. However, unlike machines, humans can be terribly inconsistent; and this fact, while often a source of delight and creativity, is also a bane to service delivery.

Barrier 2: Believing Customers Are Expendable

Since the end of World War II, the United States has been in a continual consumer growth mode, with an ever increasing demand for a wide array of goods and services. There used to be more than enough customers to go around—a seller's market. If a particular customer didn't like your service, you could usually count on there being more where that one came from.

But this is no longer true. The explosion in distribution and service outlets, from fast-food chains to travel agencies and from shopping malls to banks, has created a buyer's market. Yet most companies act as if it's business as usual, failing to recognize that the flow of customers is not endless.

This attitude that "another one will come along anyway" was demonstrated recently at a major West Coast bank. A 10-year customer with both personal and business accounts representing substantial dollars needed funds shifted from one account to the other. A mix-up occurred (cause undetermined), and the only way to rectify it was through a notarized document. The bank wanted to charge the customer $2, which on principle he didn't want to pay. Yet even the bank manager would not waive the fee. As should have been expected, the customer angrily closed all of his accounts, while making sure that other customers heard what was going on. The bank manager's response was: "Good riddance! He was a pain in the neck anyway, and we don't want his business. There are others where he came from."

There are over 14,000 banks in the United States, and major financial institutions now solicit business throughout the country, penetrating markets that locally established banks have always treated as their exclusive domains. Bankers can no longer act as though they have captive markets; there are too many competitors dipping into the same pools of customers—and those pools are by no means bottomless.

The same situation holds for any type of business. Competitors are abundant, and companies must work to earn and preserve customer loyalty.

Barrier 3: Unwillingness to Pay the Price

Some companies "nickel-and-dime" service delivery, and the result is a halfhearted, poorly implemented, and inconsistent strategy. You often hear managers complain: "We can't afford to hire more qualified people." "Our budget doesn't include enough people to handle the long lines, backlog of orders, or weekend crowds." "We can only provide *so* much service." Yet it is exactly this kind of misplaced austerity that drives many customers away in disgust at the company's cheapness.

Budgetary problems, of course, can be real. The irony is that financial resources to improve service often exist but are being allocated elsewhere in excessive proportions. Organizations that are top-heavy with management are prime examples. The salaries of unnecessary layers of management could pay for substantial customer service improvements and retention programs. The retailing and service industries are notorious for wide imbalances between management salaries and worker wages. Executives, who are furthest removed from customer contact, receive attractive salaries and bonuses, while frontline employees, who can have the most impact on customer satisfaction, typically earn little more than the minimum wage. Such a pay structure inherently devalues the importance of customer service, and that message is all too clear to employees in the trenches.

The misallocation of financial resources is a widespread problem in many industries. Phillip Crosby, author of several books on quality including *Quality Is Free*, describes one company whose assembly line was operated almost solely by women. The women repeatedly requested lockers for their personal belongings, but management refused, not wanting to spend the money. Later, under a new quality process, management recanted, installed the lockers, and suddenly saw the assembly line's productivity double! It was learned afterwards that the women, without benefit of lockers, were constantly taking their eyes off their work to look down at the floor and check on their purses, thus slowing production on the assembly line. This story is a perfect example of false economy, and its lesson is just as valid for service delivery as it is for manufacturing.

Frontline employees in retailing and services have a unique perspective on customer wants and needs, but they are often powerless to use that perspective constructively because management has failed to allocate enough money for the things that can help employees deliver good customer service.

Customer service costs money—but money is often better spent on keeping the customers you already have than on trying to attract new ones.

Customer service also is never finished; there is no such thing as a "completed" customer service program that has been bought and paid for. Both short-term and long-term benefits of good customer service can be achieved only through an ongoing commitment to paying the price.

Barrier 4: Superficial Commitments

It takes an organization-wide commitment to deliver superior customer service—a commitment from every person in the company, starting at the top. Senior management, operations, human resources, finance, marketing, and sales are all parts of the foundation of service delivery.

Top executives of companies that are truly service-oriented are unflagging in their organization-wide approach to service. They understand what commitment means and why each and every customer is important. Even the chairmen and presidents of such companies regularly visit the shop floor, sort packages, or sell merchandise. At any given time, they know what their service and sales levels are and they have a feel for what their customers are thinking.

The former chairman and CEO of a large cable television group began his leadership tenure at the company with an openly superficial attitude toward customer service. More involved with the financial and technical sides of the business, he was quoted as saying during an employee meeting in the company's early days that "service is nothing more than a smile."

As the returns came in, however, it was clear that customers were voting a different opinion; the company's service was notoriously bad, and not many people were smiling.

The chairman learned also that turning the situation around was not to be an easy task. It would take a full-scale effort and require an intense commitment at all levels of management, as well as throughout the organization.

One measure he took—and one which cost a considerable amount—was to enroll the entire senior management team in a quality college in Florida. When these people returned, they worked with the chairman to sculpt a set of common standards for each of the 150 cable systems in the company. These standards covered such things as phone-answering quality, promptness and time spent in hook-up and repair calls, billing accuracy, complaint handling, customer turnover, and a variety of other matters. The chairman reviewed monthly statistics and discussed problems with his managers either in person or through conference calls. He gave his personal attention to many customer complaints and opened every staff meeting with a complaint-handling or quality story. He allocated money to an ongoing quarterly customer survey and used the survey results as part of the basis for evaluating managers' performances. In addition, he launched a quality newsletter for distribution to all employees.

The short-term payout from all these efforts included a 20-percent decrease in customer churn, higher customer satisfaction with phone answering, better on-time service reliability, and reduced service outages. Through four years of this type of stewardship, the company developed a reputation for superior service, and it was then sold for nearly four times its original purchase price.

In any organization of more than two people, there is a chain; and in business, each link in that chain represents a potential breakdown point in service delivery. A floral shop depends upon the grower for healthy flowers, on the delivery service for timely delivery and prevention of damage in transit, on the refrigeration company for proper storage, on the backroom employees for correct handling, and on the sales clerk for an honest, courteous transaction with the customer. Each function along the way, from the field to the showcase, must be executed perfectly, or the entire process can break down. As the saying goes, any chain is only as strong as its weakest link. Service programs, therefore, must be comprehensive and must address *all* of the operational and service issues of each step throughout the delivery process, treating them as interconnecting and interdependent parts of a whole.

Barrier 5: Listening But Not Hearing; Looking But Not Seeing

Many service deficiencies can be blamed largely, if not solely, on management's failure to hear and see what's really going on with customers and employees. Managers may listen and think they're hearing; they may look and think they're seeing. But their presumptions and biases often blind and deafen them to reality.

Some managers are hooked on a technique called "management by walking around." The assumption is that if you get out there and mingle with the customers and employees, you will automatically be inspired with important insights; and in the meantime, you're "making a presence" that will presumably motivate employees and impress customers. Granted, it *is* important for managers at all levels, including senior executives, to get out from behind their desks as often as possible and observe the frontline action first hand. For example, Corning chairman James R. Houghton visits all 50 of his company's far-flung operations at least once a year to discuss product and process quality with local managers and employees.

When executives do get out and about, they should have a clear purpose, like Houghton's concentration on quality. Rather than merely "walking around" or making a presence, they need to look and listen systematically and purposefully. Furthermore, they can't be shy about having their illusions shattered.

Self-delusion in management is more commonplace than we like to admit. Managers, who are typically burdened with the "big" issues of business and simultaneously beset by swarms of pesky details, often find it comfortable to cite what are believed to be important business axioms: "Don't rock the boat." "If it isn't broke, don't fix it." "If customers aren't complaining, we must be doing all right."

But these presumed truisms aren't necessarily true. TARP claims that for every written complaint there are an average of 27 dissatisfied customers, 26 of whom did not take the trouble to write. Thus, if a company gets 100 complaint letters in a year, this represents as many as 2,700 unhappy customers. And *that* is not "doing all right."

The tendency of some managers to sweep problems under the rug is almost childlike, conjuring up images of a kid who receives a bad report card in elementary school. Bad news—customer complaints—are believed to reflect on their abilities and even on their character. Therefore, they deny that a problem exists. Yet the fact that a customer complains to a manager about a rude or unhelpful phone representative should be viewed as a positive, not a negative. Customers, in fact, have done managers a great favor, much like telling them that they have flat tires. After the bad news, what's really important is how the manager responds. Will it be indignant defensiveness? Will a band-aid be slapped on the problem? Or will the manager see that an honest, thoughtful, and systematic effort is made to correct the shortcoming? It all depends ultimately on whether the manager really absorbed what the customer was saying.

How many of us have dined in a busy restaurant and started "managing" it in our heads? "I'd hire another busboy, keep the soup hotter, train the waitress to carry more than one item per trip, or move the cash register away from the door." Of course, nobody has asked you for your opinion, and experience tells you that they probably wouldn't listen anyway. So you've simply had one more unsatisfactory dining experience, and you leave without comment. Maybe you just never go back to that place, and maybe you also tell a few friends why you don't go there anymore.

What if restaurants were denied food permits unless they independently surveyed customers and maintained a certain level of service? What if department stores were required to report average line delays or rates of merchandise returns on advertisements? What if publicly held companies had to produce audited *service* statements along with audited financial statements? It is pretty safe to say that, under these circumstances, companies in those industries would start listening to their customers very seriously.

Listening is not really all that difficult. However, in business it does require some financial resources, time, and an understanding of the right questions to ask. Business listening also requires a willingness to acknowledge the truth.

Thus, management by walking around is useless. It is too easy to delude yourself that you are learning something about the customer experience merely by walking around. A great many management tours are visiting-dignitary trips anyway. Everything is cleaned up, employees are hyped, and the executive gets the red-carpet treatment. Or, at times, managers visit with only their best customer. Such behavior is actually a slap in the face for employees and customers. The message is, "Show management your best, but give customers the usual."

Barrier 6: Using Assembly-Line Principles for Service Delivery

Consumer goods bought off the shelf are judged by their appearance, taste, durability, or a hundred other physical attributes. The buyer is not concerned about the condition of the factory where the product was made, how the line workers dress or behave, or whether they chew gum, talk with their friends, or are functionally illiterate. Customers measure a product by the satisfaction they expect to get from it.

In the delivery of service, however, a gum-chewing, chatty employee will irritate most customers because the service delivery *is* the product. The service-provider, unlike the product-producer, carries the burden of *being* what is bought. Service is the ultimate just-in-time inventory system. If a frontline service worker is poorly trained, dressed sloppily, unmotivated, or using antiquated equipment, then the service is bad. And, since we judge a service by its deliverer, a hotel bell captain with a dirty uniform is as damaging as a hot dog containing bone chips. A cashier who cannot make change will hurt the service business as much as a washing machine with a faulty motor will hurt the reputation of its manufacturer.

Service standards often refer to 90-percent accuracy as an acceptable level of performance. But why shouldn't the goal of customer service be to deliver at a 100-percent level, 100 percent of the time? Nine out of ten, or even 99 out of 100, should not be tolerated. This less-than-100-percent acceptability level in service delivery is a concept borrowed from the manufacturing and finance industries. Customers have become statistics: Two-hundred thousand diners served, 85-percent hotel occupancy rates, 25,000 cars serviced, 8,000 athletic club memberships renewed. The individual has gotten lost in a sea of numbers.

The proper approach, to borrow a sports cliche, is to "take them one game at a time." That means one service provided to one customer, then another service to another customer, and so on—with each service constituting a complete experience. The vision of a continuous stream of customers can have a numbing effect on employees, which is why it's important to instill the "one-game-at-a-time" attitude. The key issue is that one failure in 100 transactions is the same as a *100-percent problem* for *one customer*. Likewise, 90-percent accuracy on 100,000 bills translates into 10,000 customers with inaccurate accounts—10,000 unhappy customers who will probably have to call, come in, or write to straighten out a mistake that probably wasn't their fault.

There is a dehumanizing effect in serving hundreds of customers a day. Employees tend to think of themselves as robots and make customers feel as if they are on an assembly line. This often accounts for the employee's glazed look, the sagging posture, and the monotone "Who's next please?" We have learned that there are economies of scale in servicing multitudes of customers—the more the better—but we have not been able to strike a good balance between mass production service and personal service, between high tech and high touch. We have forgotten that a customer is not a line on a graph, a digit on a sales report, or a component on an assembly line. And we've forgotten, too, that the customer plays an active, elective role in any transaction or instance of service delivery.

Barrier 7: Quality Service Is Hard to Define and Measure

What, exactly, *is* high-quality service? Is it like beauty or art—in the eye of the beholder? Is it like obscenity or pornography insofar as you simply "know it when I see it"? Or can it be defined in concrete, objective terms?

Actually, the definition of quality service is as elusive as the concept of customer satisfaction. It means different things to different people at different times and places. Yet in every business, management must identify those service attributes that work best for its customers and that can act as guideposts for measurable improvement. The difficulty is that most of the terms used to describe service attributes are general or ambiguous. We use words like "professional," "courtesy," "consistent," "prompt," "reliable," and, of course, "satisfaction." But these words have an almost endless variety of meanings, depending upon the circumstances in which they're used. For purposes of defining, measuring, and managing the delivery of service, they are practically useless. Even such generally understood attributes as accuracy in billing, quick response to complaints, adequate staffing during rush hours, and prompt repairs are nebulous unless you have some concrete standard to measure them against.

What's needed are *specific* measurements such as 24-hour response time to complaints, customers in line for no more than ten minutes at any time, four-hour repair service, and other explicitly stated standards. Every company should survey its customers to identify the service standards important to them and then measure the gap between customer expectation and reality. Continuous improvement is the watchword. If the standard for resolving complaints is now at 80 percent, then next year the target should be 85 percent; and it is important to monitor and measure your progress toward that targeted standard.

One hotel had a specific 10-point room-condition checklist including such standards as correctly made beds, three towels in the bathroom, the provision of other bathroom items, presence of room-service menu, vacuumed carpets, and so on. Random inspections were done, and the inspector from housekeeping came with ten $1 bills in an envelope for each room. Each time one of the checklist standards was not met, a dollar was removed from the envelope, and the money remaining in the envelope after the inspection was completed was given to the service person who had cleaned that room.

Another hotel had small cards made up that said, "You clean under your bed, so do we." One of these cards was placed under the bed in each room before a guest arrived, and it was amazing how many guests found the cards.

Depending upon what business you're in, there are hundreds or thousands of points where things can go wrong in serving the customer. Let's look, for example, at a retail appliance company that does installation and repairs, and let's consider just seven service points where installers and repair specialists can please or displease the customer: (1) promptness of arrival, (2) knowledge of the job, (3) personal appearance and demeanor, (4) length of stay, (5) verbal communications with the customer, (6) quality of the work, and (7) thoroughness of cleanup after the job. If the company has 10 installers and repair specialists, each making 50 calls per month, this works out to at least 3,500 ($7 \times 10 \times 50$) service-delivery points per month where things can go wrong. And that's just for the actual at-home service calls. The number gets even larger when you add all the other customer-service points involving such people as phone answerers, sales clerks, secretaries, and bill processors.

Seen in such specific terms, the enormity of the challenge becomes obvious. But at least the concept of "quality" has begun to take on concrete, measurable dimensions. It is more feasible to pinpoint areas where quality might be compromised.

Barrier 8: The Protective Shield of Policies, Procedures, and Protocol

Few experiences can be more frustrating to a consumer than hearing the words: "I'm sorry, but our policy is . . ." or, "I understand how you feel, but there's nothing I can do about it."

Procedure manuals, policy guides, and computer systems are an unholy trinity that take on a life of their own in many companies. Like alien spirits, they infiltrate the organization and manipulate people's minds until the weakened and submissive organization is at their mercy. No action is taken and no decision is made without first consulting this mighty triumvirate. Customers become fodder for the machine to chew up and spit out if they do not behave as the system demands. The policy guide at most companies is huge and is used as if it were a suit of armor to protect the organization from customer flak. Procedure manuals are typically complicated and so filled with company jargon that they can be used to justify almost anything that goes wrong or refute any claim that a customer may have. The computer system can also be used as a handy excuse for foul-ups, and managers and employees alike can have their thought processes virtually narcotized by dependency upon the EDP system. Kenneth Leach of Globe Metallurgical says that a key part of his company's quality strategy is to "avoid computer complacency." The computer is a cost-effective tool for Globe's manufacturing processes that involve extremely close tolerances and delicate measurements, but managers and employees still use their own eyes, ears, and brains to see that the job gets done right.

As managers rise through the ranks, their attitudes change. They often feel that they have "paid their dues" and now deserve a more hands-off job. Some managers may not have worked directly with customers a day in their lives, having moved from business school to management with no line experience. The job focus for these people is in the numbers, the logistics, and the "things" of the business. Customers are little more than phantoms—or worse, blips on a computer screen.

Organizational protocol is a serious stumbling block to customer service in many companies. Management is too removed from the place where profit is really made, where customers decide to stay or to leave, to buy or not to buy. Sometimes, managers need to become imposters, posing as real customers and be willing to experience what actually happens when customers come into contact with their company's policies and procedures. How often does a company president anonymously walk into a branch office, store, or ticket counter and try to revise an incorrect bill or otherwise sample the customer service being delivered by the company? Unflattering as it might be, most employees would not recognize the president if he or she walked in unannounced.

Management's time is typically consumed by budgets, reports, memos, luncheons, policy reviews, meetings, phone calls, and other such executive chores. In this hubbub of activity, a single-minded focus on customer service is difficult to maintain. All the other tasks take on a life of their own and blur a company's true mission: to sell and to service the customer.

This confusion over mission accounts for the widening gap between those who lead a company and those who service its customers. Companies that excel at service never waver in their focus and never allow "the system" to interfere with customer interests. The majority of their time and resources is devoted to the pursuit of serving the customer better, even if the computer doesn't agree or the policy manual doesn't have a clause to cover the situation.

Old ways of doing things are comfortable to most people.

Established policies, communication channels, and rules of protocol give managers and employees a sense of identity and stability, even though they may also stifle initiative. Any time you try to change the old ways, you'll most likely run into objections. Robert Galvin of Motorola says that when his company began to formulate its new quality program, there was strong resistance: "Motorola was number one in our industry in market share, sales, and profits at the time. However, our product quality really *stunk*, and we had to do something about it."

Galvin called a top-management meeting that was to last three full days and to be focused intensely on the issue of quality. He recalls, "But people said we shouldn't spend the time or money on such a thing. That happened to be during the hard times of 1978, and many of our officers thought we should be concentrating on day-to-day concerns like sales and finance."

Intent upon taking a longer view of quality, Galvin told his management team that Motorola had to do a lot more training. They responded, "Great, just as long as we don't spend any money or time on it." But Galvin put his foot down and said, "No, we're going to spend tens of millions, and everybody will just have to find a way to pull the money out of other budgets if that's what it takes."

Later, when Galvin put the subject of quality on the agenda for *every* monthly meeting of the firm's operating committee, there was continued resistance. According to Galvin, "People wanted to talk about everything *but* quality. They didn't relate quality to other operations and issues such as finance and sales." Eventually, and with his persistence, the company's executives started coming around. "It took a while," he adds, "but gradually, people started warming up and seeing quality in relation to everything else we did. Then they started getting really excited."

On a different level, the Ford Motor Company experienced similar resistance when it launched its recovery program. Hourly workers and line supervisors were not only skeptical but, in some cases, derisive when top management talked about building new "world-class" cars. It took persistent management effort and courageous support from forward-thinking union officials to convince people that the company was serious and that the job *could* be done. American automaking had always been hidebound in its thinking and methods—perhaps more so than many other industries—and the task of changing attitudes and values was a huge challenge. Even in 1989, the National Automobile Dealers Association criticized manufacturers' attempts to survey retail customers on service satisfaction. The dealers felt that such studies were potentially embarrassing and threatening to them as independent businesses.

Many people view change in their work lives as at least unsettling, if not actually threatening, and this built-in resistance can be a serious barrier to improving quality and customer satisfaction. Old policies, procedures, and ways of thinking die hard, and it takes courage and ingenuity to successfully challenge them.

Barrier 9: Preoccupation with Short-Term Results

A total quality-improvement effort requires changing the company's entire culture, and that takes both money and time. Ford committed $5 billion and took five years to recover from the brink of disaster and to achieve world-class product quality and record profitability. Yet in 1989, nine years after the start of Ford's turnaround, chairman Donald Petersen said the company was only about 20 percent of the way to its goal and that Ford's official policy now is "*continuous* improvement."

Other major companies that are engaged in successful quality programs—companies such as Motorola, Westinghouse Nuclear Fuels, and Corning Glass Works—report that it takes anywhere from four to five years to revolutionize quality once management has made the commitment to do everything that's necessary. For smaller companies, such as Globe Metallurgical, the time frame may be somewhat condensed but still significant, and the investment is proportionately the same. When new management launched a total quality program at Globe, it took two years to achieve spectacular results. In 1985, the company had forty-four customer complaints and slightly more than 2 percent of defective products returned. In 1987, there were just *four* complaints and *zero* returns. Over that same two-year period, Globe went from 5 percent to 50 percent share of market in ductile iron and won the highest preferred supplier awards given by Ford and General Motors.

Whether it took Ford five years or Globe two years to achieve award-winning quality is not the central issue. Management of any size company may commit to time-framed programs to meet specified goals or reach certain levels of improvement, but high quality and good service really require an *unending* commitment.

John Marous of Westinghouse describes total quality as a "process" and adds that Westinghouse's long-run mission is quality *perfection*. Robert Galvin of Motorola says his company's driving thrust is "renewal." Quality became the first order of business at Motorola a decade ago, and the company expects to reach what it calls "virtual perfection" by 1992. "Ironically," says Galvin, "from then on, we will still find better ways. Quality has become *the* way of life for most of us at Motorola, and it *will* be for *all* of us."

These are the winners talking, and what they're saying is that quality improvement is an ongoing job that shouldn't be confused with or controlled by short-term objectives. With the outside financial community or shareholders looking over their shoulders, most CEOs and financial officers typically focus on immediate and visible profits. Others in the company set short-term goals for sales, productivity rates, cost-cutting, or any number of other activities that are seen as important from an internal perspective or in the best interests of a particular division or department of the company. Certainly, there are times when it's necessary to take short-range steps to solve an immediate problem, but no such actions should be taken unless they are compatible with the overall, continuing mission of creating better value for customers.

Barrier 10: Overselling

If you own or manage a business, you've got to appreciate the people who bring in your customers and close the sales, and if you're a salesperson yourself, you belong to a special club where outstanding sales ability is admired, respected, and even revered. But if you're a customer who's been sold on a product or service that doesn't live up to the salesperson's promises, you can find yourself muttering about stereotypes of "hucksters" and "snake-oil salesmen."

From management's standpoint, the problem goes deeper and lasts longer. Customers who have been oversold or promised undeliverable satisfaction tend to quickly forget the salesperson and focus on the product or service. The seller, after all, was "only doing his or her job," but the bad product remains or the memory of unsatisfactory service lingers; thus, the unhappy experience ultimately is associated with the company behind the sale or the brand name of the product.

It's tempting to say that the solution is simply to teach salespeople not to oversell. But that's unrealistic in many cases because it's hard to draw the line at just where the overselling occurs, and the last thing a company wants to do is dampen the enthusiasm of its sales force.

Nonetheless, overselling is at the root of many customer-service problems, and companies need to constantly monitor what their salespeople are promising customers. If the promises are patently untrue, then some sort of penalty or disciplinary action is clearly in order. If the overselling is more subtle or is the result of genuine but exaggerated enthusiasm, the issue becomes stickier.

Any company that's dedicated to total quality, however, will find ways to bring its sales personnel into the quality process. Salespeople, as much as any other members of the organization, have to be encouraged and taught to think in terms of long-term results and customer loyalty.

The barriers discussed above are by no means an exhaustive, all-inclusive list of the impediments to good service. But they and others have defeated even the best-intentioned companies—companies whose management really wanted to do the job right. And while barriers can be analyzed and written about in great detail, that merely speaks to the problems. The cold fact is that consistent, effective service delivery is hard to develop and hard to maintain. It requires first of all a fundamental shift in priorities and then a persistent top-of-mind awareness and unflagging attention to detail. And while these attitudinal changes are being effected, someone has to start coming up with creative solutions for individual service problems. As one executive once said: "I'll give you two points for identifying the problem, and you'll get the other eight when you bring me the solution."

Id the problem   2 points
Solution   8 points

3

PRACTICAL WAYS
TO KEEP
YOUR CUSTOMERS

WE'VE LOOKED at the common barriers to good customer service. Now let's look at some of the specific actions that can overcome those barriers.

Most of what follows is a matter of plain common sense. But as simple as these steps may seem, many of them are often overlooked or never fully understood. Some managers get too busy "doing business" to pay attention to these basic principles; they manage everything but the fundamentals of keeping customers happy. Others make the task too complicated; they exaggerate the difficulty of satisfying customers and look for "sophisticated" solutions.

None of the following steps, taken alone or in concert, are guaranteed formulas for solving service problems, but all of them are sensible, workable methods. Neither is this collection of ideas the final word on customer satisfaction. You, the reader, may add any number of ideas that you've developed yourself or learned from other sources. What's important is to get out of the idea stage and into action. Start putting these and other methods to work. The company or the job they save may be your own.

Select Customer-Contact Employees Carefully

Many employees in customer-contact jobs are ill-suited by nature to deal with people. They may be trained to work the cash register, know the merchandise, and parrot the words, "May I help you, please?" and "Thank you." But they lack the outgoing personality, enthusiasm, and honest desire to serve. In the banking business, for example, many tellers are hired mainly for their ability to handle figures accurately and quickly, but they may be like robots in dealing with customers.

Companies that are truly service-oriented know it's absolutely essential to have customer-friendly people on the front lines, and they take great care in screening prospective employees for appropriate personality traits as well as other skills. Outside consulting firms can use proven psychological methods to help you develop customized employee-assessment programs, pre-employment screening techniques, and hiring models. Some larger companies have in-house resources to do the same things for themselves. Piedmont Airlines, for example, studied its frontline employees who had consistently high customer service performance reviews, and isolated their common personality traits. The company then developed tests based upon these traits to reassess other employees with lower performance records and to screen new applicants. Among the personal attributes singled out for attention were the ability to make sound judgments under stress, a desire to be liked, a problem-solving mindset, and a naturally optimistic outlook. Piedmont also produced interactive videotape programs presenting realistic on-the-job problems and had employees and applicants demonstrate how they would handle such situations. For example, what would a customer service agent at the boarding gate do with a child traveling alone if the flight were cancelled?

Piedmont has had good results from its overall program of screening, evaluating, and role playing. Other companies can use similar methods to ensure better initial selection and continuing review of front-line employees.

Employee Training Is the Company's Job—Not the Customer's

Employees should be well-trained *before* being put in front of customers or assigned to other customer-contact jobs such as phone answering. On-the-job training may be an inexpensive way of breaking in new employees, but it also makes the customer share the training burden. Customers want to be served by knowledgeable personnel, not by somebody wearing an "In-Training" badge or hat. They want to get what they came for without having to stumble through a trial-and-error exercise with a poorly prepared trainee.

There is a place for on-the-job training in customer service, but it's at the very end of the initial training process. It's the point where thoroughly prepared new employees get their first test under fire—with more experienced or supervisory personnel nearby to help out if necessary and ensure that the customer isn't mishandled.

At Federal Express, new employees are trained for as long as six weeks before they ever deal directly with customers. This costs about $1,800 per employee, but Federal Express cannot afford to teach employees under fire because the company's most important product is *reliability*. There simply isn't room for the kinds of errors that spanking-new, untrained employees would inevitably make.

On-the-job-training can also perpetuate bad habits. Employees, especially new ones, take their cues from their immediate bosses and from other senior personnel in their work groups. If the bosses and older personnel got their training on the job and acquired bad habits in the process, the newer employees will be caught in a continuing cycle of poor performance.

Help Employees Feel As If They Really Belong

Everybody would like to have loyal, dedicated employees who are proud to be a part of the company. This takes a special attitude and commitment from top management as well as a continuous effort throughout the middle ranks.

Conventional "involvement" and "employee support" programs include such extracurricular activities as company-sponsored bowling and softball teams, picnics, Christmas parties, awards banquets, and employee committees to promote local causes or special interests. But employees also need a sense of their company's real mission, and they need to be encouraged to enhance their own roles at work.

Disneyland employees, from the beginning of their orientation and training period, are totally immersed in the theme park's traditions, mission, and customer values. No job at Disneyland is too menial or insignificant to be a part of the show, and all employees are taught to be enthusiastic members of the cast.

Ford Motor Company production workers have their Employee Involvement Program that's designed not only to tap their hands-on job knowledge but also to let them know that they're truly part of the team effort.

At L. L. Bean, which sells outdoor sportswear and accessories, employees are encouraged and paid to take part in outdoor sports activities and to attend clinics and conferences on outdoor recreation. The company wants its people to know more about what they sell than merely the prices, available sizes, and what's in or out of stock.

Banc One Corporation, an Ohio-based firm with 566 banking locations and 18,000 employees in five states, concentrates heavily on employee recognition. The company

pany gives "We Care" awards to employees who have performed outstanding customer service or contributed uniquely to the total-quality program. Charles Aubrey, Banc One's chief quality officer, says, "We believe in giving people a pat on the back when they deserve it. We hold banquets and other special events where people are personally recognized for achievement; and we write about our top performers and put their pictures in company publications." Aubrey adds that, given adequate and equitable pay, such personal recognition appears to be a better motivator than financial awards. This opinion is shared by Corning's chairman, James Houghton, who says his company stopped giving financial awards for employee suggestions because such awards actually created ill feelings among workers. "The people who were paid for their suggestions usually thought they didn't get enough," says Houghton, "and other employees felt the award-winners didn't deserve what they got."

Regardless of the individual techniques used by different companies, employee recognition is a fundamental motivator and an essential tool for building a quality- and service-conscious environment.

Train, Retrain, and Then Train Some More

Expense cutting is the vogue in today's economy, and employee training and development programs are often seen as handy places to trim costs. But this is another of those false economies that keep undercutting customer service. Employees, even if they were well-trained at the start, can fall into ruts or lose sight of important service principles after they've been on the job for a while. Companies also change policies and procedures; new products are developed; competitors create new challenges; and customer needs and wants evolve with the changing marketplace. Employee training, therefore, is not a one-time job-entrance requirement. Periodic refreshers and updaters are needed to keep employees from losing touch with basic service standards and to teach them how to respond to changing conditions.

At Federal Express, package sorters are tested every three months for accuracy, and anyone who falls below the standard of 100 percent is sent back for retraining. This may seem expensive, but if a Federal Express sorter makes only one mistake in 100 tries, that single mistake may be a 100-percent disaster to the customer. Since a typical Federal Express customer is someone who uses the service repeatedly, only one missent or delayed package can cost the company an untold amount of future business.

Embassy Suites Hotels, a subsidiary of Holiday Corp., encourages newly hired and low-paid employees to take company-sponsored classes in the various skills needed to operate a hotel. Hervey Feldman, president of Embassy Suites, says hotel managers historically have felt that minimum-wage workers are not ambitious or smart enough to hold better jobs, but Feldman emphatically disagrees, saying that with good training any employee has the potential to "go beyond making beds."

Merck Sharp & Dohme, the pharmaceuticals company, puts newly hired salespeople through a three-phase, *11-month* training program, and then requires them to regularly attend medical classes at several leading universities.

Ongoing training is an essential part of any total-quality strategy. Motorola provides an average of one million hours of training yearly for its workforce of 102,000 employees, and approximately 40 percent of that training time is devoted solely to quality and service issues. A. William Wiggenhorn, Motorola's corporate vice president for training and education, says that "quality-related training begins with the highest executive levels, then cascades down to every worker in the company."

The Westinghouse Nuclear Fuels Division likewise emphasizes continuous training in its award-winning quality program. In 1988, more than 600 of the division's plant employees participated in 83 skills-development workshops.

The immediate purpose of ongoing employee training and development is to maintain high service levels and thus to keep customers. Beyond that, well-trained employees are more comfortable and confident in their jobs and tend to have greater respect and loyalty toward the company. It's been said so often that it's trite, but among today's corps of trainee-novices are many of tomorrow's managers. A new employee who has the intelligence and skills to move up through the ranks will be eager to learn and impatient with a company that doesn't offer the chance for continuous improvement. Even employees who are "topped out" or content to stay where they are will be happier and more productive if the company helps them keep their skills current and sharply honed.

Never Let Your Customers Be Guinea Pigs

On-the-job training of employees is one way to make guinea pigs of customers. Another is to take a new product or service to market before it's ready. Still others include changing policies, introducing different procedures, or launching new computer systems before all the bugs are worked out and everybody is prepared.

Test marketing of new products is a long-established research technique, but many companies still release unproven, unwanted, or defective products. Debugging new computer systems or setting up other high-tech programs are also well-known trouble spots, but companies still rush into action with the latest technology before the impact on customers is fully understood. This thinking implies, "Sure, we'll have some problems, but once we get this baby working, everybody's going to be better off." That may be true from an internal viewpoint, but how many customers must be sacrificed while the debugging and fine-tuning are going on? Customers don't want to be treated like experimental animals. If there's any important experimenting taking place, it's the customer who is testing you and your product or service.

Inform Employees about Other Parts of the Company

Once inside the front door, customers don't always know where to go or who to ask for what they want. The same is true for many phone calls; customers dial an inappropriate number from among the company's several directory listings and then have to be transferred to the right department.

Every employee on the front lines and phone lines should be able to direct customers to the right place and give them basic information in a courteous fashion. The department store lingerie clerk should know where men's wear is, and the busboy should know when the restaurant opens and closes.

Some of the best-informed employees at Disneyland are the streetsweepers. Constantly on the job and unintimidating, they are always accessible to guests who need directions or advice. They know where the nearest bathrooms, water fountains, first-aid stations, and telephones are. They know when the park closes and how long it will take you to walk back to your car from wherever you are. And they usually know what bands are playing at the various pavilions, hotels, and street corners in the park.

Most enthusiastic and dedicated employees make it their business to know all they can about the company. But management cannot assume this is true for the whole workforce. Systematic training and information programs are needed to ensure that employees can give accurate directions and advice on services outside their own departments.

In some companies it's feasible to have employees visit other departments for an hour or two each week or month until they've learned at least the rudiments of what goes on in the rest of the company. At others, employees may actually be transferred to a different department every six months or so. Periodic staff orientation meetings are also helpful, especially in companies where departments, facilities, or procedures are frequently changed. Internal newsletters, bulletins, and service directories with maps can be circulated to all employees from time to time. And for a reasonable investment, companies can produce videotaped employee "tours" showing all physical layouts and describing the activities at each location.

Whatever the medium, the message is that customers should never have to find their way through a maze or be greeted with blank stares when they ask simple questions.

Give Frontline Employees Enough Authority

Most people live up to or down to what's expected of them. On the whole, if you treat employees like responsible adults, that's what you'll get: responsible adults.

Many companies need to give frontline personnel more authority and trust them to do the jobs they were hired to do. Employees who don't respond don't belong in the job.

Both the customer and the employee are frustrated when the simplest transactions have to be monitored or approved by supervisors. The customer has to wait, and the employee is made to feel inferior. A person who shops regularly at a particular supermarket and whose face and name are well-known shouldn't have to wait for the manager to approve every check. But many supermarkets follow this same exasperating procedure for every customer who writes a check, regardless of how long the cashier has been on the job or how many checks the customer has cashed there in the past.

An employee who is otherwise qualified for the job should be trained—and trusted—to use discretion in dealing with customers. That includes giving refunds, exchanging merchandise, and handling complaints in all but the most questionable of situations. Certainly, there will be occasional mistakes at the company's cost, and some employees may have to be monitored more closely than others until they have either proven their good judgment or shown themselves to be unworthy of trust and thus unfit for the job. The objective should be to simplify matters for the customer and build confidence and competence in the employee. Many managers find it hard to give employees enough room for this to happen. But James Houghton says that "power must be transmitted downward and outward." And Forum Corporation's Richard Whitely says that a good service strategy means "empowering individuals to offer the best possible service they can, within reasonable limits."

Don't Make Customers Pay the Freight for Service

The manager of a national credit card department made the following statement at an internal company meeting not long after "800" telephone service was introduced:

> "We don't want an '800' number. It will just encourage people to call over the slightest thing, and it costs $50,000. Let the customer pay for the call."

That kind of attitude won't take you far in today's marketplace, but it's still embraced by many senior executives and business proprietors.

The installation of "800" numbers is more readily accepted if the purpose is selling or order taking because management can relate the cost directly to new business. However, the U.S. Department of Consumer Affairs reports that toll-free lines installed explicitly for customer service and complaint handling have also proven to be powerful competitive tools; and a TARP study shows that 50 percent of toll-free calls are product-information requests that represent new sales opportunities. Also, in many cases, the number and complexity of customer service problems has declined after "800" lines were installed, thus lowering the costs of complaint handling.

Toll-free lines are often less expensive than management anticipates, and, if they help keep customers, their cost should be regarded not as an overhead expense but as a marketing investment. In any case, it isn't fair to expect customers to pay for long-distance service calls. Many such calls are made because the company itself did something wrong or failed to provide the customer with adequate information. Having presented the customer with a problem, the company should now make it easy and cost-free for the customer to get the problem resolved.

Requiring customers to write or make personal trips to straighten out service problems are other ways of unfairly shifting the cost of poor service. The still-adolescent cable television industry is notorious for this. Even at the start of a new subscriber relationship, many of the smaller cable firms require that the customer come to the office and pick up the "black box" (cable-converter), despite the fact that the company's installer still has to come to the customer's home to hook up the system and deliver the remote-control tuner. But that's only for starters. If the converter and tuner aren't compatible, or either of them doesn't work properly, many companies require that the customer bring the equipment back to the office to be exchanged or repaired. And, in defiance of all reason, some companies even charge the customer's account for a "service" call when defective or malfunctioning equipment has to be brought back.

Banks can be guilty of such service myopia, too. A bank customer recently discovered a 20-cent error in the bank's favor on his checking-account statement, and he phoned the bank about it. There was no question that the bank was at fault, and while 20 cents won't buy even a pack of gum anymore, the customer felt the error should be corrected. If the bank's key punchers could enter a 20-cent mistake and the system didn't catch it, the next time it could be a $20 or $2,000 error—enough to make checks start bouncing. However, the bank's customer service representative couldn't or wouldn't deal with the problem over the phone. She told the customer to bring his statement to the bank or make a copy and mail it. The customer replied that it would take at least 50 cents worth of gas for the 15-mile roundtrip between his home and the bank, or 10 cents for a photocopy and 25 cents postage to mail a copy of the statement. This certainly wasn't high finance, but it seemed incredible that the bank expected the *customer* to spend more to fix its *own* error than the error was worth—and that didn't even take into account the customer's time.

Many such cases of making the customer pay for poor service arise from company policies that are outdated, clumsy, or inflexible. Others occur because nobody is paying attention to the little details. Some are the result of outright greed. But *all* reflect a serious disregard for the value of customers.

Make Everything Easy for the Customer

Whether a toll-free long-distance line is involved or not, customer service "help lines" should be available explicitly to handle complaints, answer questions, and furnish added information about products and services. Multiple help lines feeding off of a single phone number should be amply staffed with well-trained and customer-friendly personnel who are able and authorized to take prompt, effective action. Customers should not have to be put on hold or be shunted through several departments to find answers to their problems.

Likewise, in-store or on-premises information desks and complaint departments should be set up to provide customers easy access, prompt attention, comfort, and pleasant surroundings. No customer should ever be made to feel unsure, embarrassed, or pressured when lodging a complaint.

There are hundreds of other ways in which any company can make it easy for customers to do business with it. Postage-prepaid return mail is an example of simplifying customer communications. The customer not only is pleased at getting the free postage but also appreciates not having to go through the fussy little routine of searching the house for a stamp and then licking it and sticking it on an envelope.

Internal procedures for merchandise exchanges and refunds can be simplified in any retail store. There's no excuse for a customer to have to go to one department for a credit slip, another department for a refund approval, and back to the sales counter or a cashier's station to complete the transaction.

Some department stores go to great lengths to make shopping easy. At one West Coast chain, when a customer buys a suit, sales clerks routinely make the rounds of different departments to gather assortments of accessories such as ties, shirts, and belts to go with the suit. Clerks also take the customer's place in line at the fitting room while the customer continues shopping.

Making things easy for the customer requires intelligent planning, coordination, and constant attention. When companies don't work hard at these fundamentals, the results can sometimes be incredible. Here's a recent horror story from a customer of a major insurance company—a company that promotes itself as being highly sensitive and responsive to individual customer needs. The customer in this case needed to file a claim, so she drove to a nearby branch office that had a prominently displayed "Drive-Through Claims" sign. Not being in a big hurry, she parked, went inside the office, and asked for a claims agent. The young clerk at the front desk told her, however, that claims could be filed only by appointment and that she would have to call another office to make such an appointment. The customer asked why all this was necessary when the sign outside advertised drive-through claim service; and the clerk responded, "Those drive-through windows aren't open all the time, and it's a lot of trouble to keep taking the sign down and putting it up again." The customer then took the phone number for the other office, went home, and placed the call to make an appointment. When her call was answered, she began by giving her policy number, but the man's voice at the other end interrupted her, saying, "Don't bother giving me that, because I don't have a computer." She was then put on hold and spent several minutes listening to elevator music while waiting to talk with a real claims agent who, presumably, would be computer-equipped. Eventually, the original man's voice came back on the line; he told her she could leave a message, and someone would "get back to her." All of this happened in mid-morning, and the customer spent the rest of the day at home, with her telephone in good working order; but nobody from the insurance company called her back that day or the next. She eventually went to the company's main local office—a 20-mile roundtrip from her home—and spent more than an hour getting her claim filed. As soon as she received a check some two weeks later, she cashed it and then wrote the company a letter cancelling all three policies she'd been carrying with that company for a number of years. It's probably safe to assume, too, that she told a number of friends about how "sensitive and responsive" this company really is toward its customers.

Beware of Rigid or Outdated Policies and Procedures

A daughter who had helped her mother prepare Thanksgiving dinner for several years, finally asked why the mother always cut off the end of the ham before putting it in the oven. "Well," said the mother, "It must make the ham cook better. Anyway, that's what my own mother always did." Not satisfied with this answer, the daughter called her grandmother and asked the same question. "Oh," said the grandmother, "That's just the way you do it. *My* mother did it that way, too." Next the daughter went to the resthome to see her 90-year-old great-grandmother and asked, "Granny, why do you have to cut off the end of a ham before you cook it? Mom and grandma told me that's how *you* always did it." The great-grandmother puckered her brows for a moment and then got a twinkle in her eyes. "Land's sake," she said, "I just never had a big enough pan, so I had to cut off part of the ham to make it fit."

That's the way it is with a lot of company policies and procedures. They were adopted because at one time they fit a particular situation; but today that situation may not exist, and nobody has taken the trouble to reexamine the need.

Policies and procedures are necessary to hold an organization together and to furnish guidelines for getting things done. But they can also be used as convenient excuses for not having to think, and if they're allowed to take on lives of their own or become ends in themselves, they can be dangerous enemies to good sense.

In many companies, policies and procedures have become serious impediments to good customer service. The corporate policy manual may not have been updated for years, and day-to-day procedures have become inflexible rules that allow employees no latitude in dealing with individual customer needs.

Speak English—Not "Companyese"

> Clerk to customer: "I'm sorry, sir, but we can't pair up your 405 with our Recon Exception form, so you'll have to file an RFR with Admin Group at the Op Center."
> Customer: "No kidding!"

Remember that customers haven't spent years working for your company and aren't privy to your special codes and jargon. Insider language is for insiders only. When you talk to customers, you have to speak in plain English, and all written matter such as letters, forms, and instructional pieces have to be written in plain English.

Don't Assume Too Much Knowledge on the Customer's Part

In banking these days, there's a great proliferation of product—a bewildering array of accounts, services, financial instruments, and "special" programs—with each bank having its own lexicon of marketing-inspired or jargonized names for its grab bag of products. It can all be very confusing to customers, especially to those who are switching banks.

One customer recently moved to a different state and opened new checking, passbook-savings, and money-market accounts with a local bank. All three accounts were linked together to give the customer free checking, a good interest rate on savings, overdraught protection, and a checking-account cash withdrawal card for the 24-hour automated teller machine. However, the first time the customer tried to get cash from the machine, there was a problem. After she punched all the normal information, including her 10-digit and 16-digit account numbers, onto the touch-screen, the machine printed out a question: "What type of checking account do you have? Organized Checking? Or Checking II?" Neither of those terms meant anything to her. She didn't recall the bank clerk distinguishing between them when her accounts were opened, and she couldn't remember seeing either name on her monthly statement. No reason to worry, though, because surely the plastic card would tell what kind of account it was. Except that it didn't. Needing the cash, the customer decided to make an educated guess, although she wondered why, if there was a "Checking II," there wasn't also a "'Checking I." Finally, she picked "Organized Checking" for no reason except that it sounded good—and she got her money.

There are several reasons why this customer was inconvenienced. First, the bank's nomenclature isn't compatible with the way customers think and talk. Second, the bank clerk who sold the customer the package of accounts didn't clearly impress upon her the type of checking account she was getting. Third, the name of the account should be printed on the cash-withdrawal card. And fourth, the bank's computer system ought to be able to identify the type of account by the account number, which would make it unnecessary for the teller machine to ask the question.

Most of the time, customers don't know as much about your product or service as you do, and they don't understand how your company operates. There's a danger in talking down to customers or treating them in a patronizing way, but you should tactfully make sure that they know all they need to know. Never assume that they will always ask the right questions or tell you their real problems. And never take it for granted that they know where to go to get what they want.

Use the Sunset Rule for Complaint Handling

When a customer has a problem, don't let the sun set that day without doing *something* about it. If the problem can't be totally resolved on the spot or "before the sun goes down," you should at least set the process in motion and let the customer know that you're taking action. It may require only making a phone call or writing a letter to reassure the customer that somebody's paying attention. The important rule is that no customer should ever be left waiting and wondering.

Treat Customer Complaints as Opportunities to Do Better

A complaint-handling department can be viewed as a profit center if the company treats customer complaints as opportunities rather than threats. In fact, the U.S. Office of Consumer Affairs reports that complaint departments can earn a return on investment of 15 to more than 100 percent, depending upon how well the company follows up in resolving customers' problems.

Every complaint is actually a valuable piece of business intelligence. It tells you that something is wrong and has to be fixed. Not only does this intelligence report allow you to save a current customer, it also reveals an imperfection that can lead to continuing problems.

For these reasons, complaint departments should be managed by high-level personnel who report to senior management, and periodic reviews should be conducted to track and analyze the sources and causes of complaints.

Sometimes a complaint from only one customer is actually the tip of an iceberg, and there are many more customers who have the same problem but haven't reported it to you. If the company routinely tracks and evaluates its complaints, there is an opportunity to reach out to those silently dissatisfied customers and make them happy again. L. L. Bean did this after it sold a number of shirts that were improperly fitted by the manufacturer. A single customer complaint triggered an evaluation, and when the company learned that most of the shirts in that vendor shipment were poorly fitted, it took the initiative of offering a refund or exchange opportunity to *everybody* who had bought the shirts.

In some companies, customer dissatisfaction can be anticipated before the complaints come in, and firms can take advance steps to demonstrate their concern for customer satisfaction. This, in effect, is a public relations and marketing strategy. A Canadian airline, for example, automatically sends mailgram apologies to its frequent fliers whenever a flight doesn't take off or arrive on schedule. Nobody waits for complaints. The mailgrams are prepared and sent as soon as the flight delay occurs, and many times they arrive at the passengers' homes before the passengers do.

Don't Forget That Compliments Are Important Too

All of us like a pat on the back when we deserve it. Whenever a company receives compliments from its customers, those compliments should be disseminated for the benefit of employee morale and as verification to management of what the firm is doing right. If you know through complimentary customer feedback that something is working well, you might want to further strengthen that particular service or procedure. A compliment could also save you from junking or weakening a service whose benefit was in doubt. Management may have been thinking, "This is too much trouble; it costs too much and doesn't mean anything to customers anyway." If the company systematically surveys customer opinion, this shouldn't be a problem. If not, then a timely compliment brought to management's attention can prevent a mistake.

Doing It Right the First Time Saves Money and Customers

Research shows that, in manufacturing, the cost of *not* doing the job right the first time represents 25 to 35 percent of a company's total expenses. Money is wasted because defective products have to be scrapped or repaired, and customers are lost when bad products get through the system and on the market without being detected.

In the retailing and service industries, where there is more personal contact between the company and customer, the cost of not doing a job right the first time jumps to as much as 50 percent of the total budget. Having a poor service strategy not only chases away customers but also causes more employee turnover, leading in turn to bigger hiring and training expense. Bad service also encourages more merchandise returns and refunds, eats up supervisors' time, and creates the need for more "firefighting" personnel such as phone answerers and complaint handlers.

Ultimately, customers are forced to pay for poor service because companies raise prices to cover the excess costs. On the other hand, if a company does the job right the first time, it will have lower costs and will be able to offer more competitive prices. In the latter case, everybody wins.

Treat Every Customer Like a Long-Term Investment

Most customers begin with a blank slate whenever they do business with a company for the first time. There are no bad experiences and no good ones—just expectations— and those expectations can be fragile opportunities for the company because it they're not met at the beginning, the customer may never come back. Even customers who try for a second or third time won't go on being disappointed indefinitely. Each time an expectation goes unmet, the customer's inclination to try again drops off exponentially.

Remember: You've invested heavily in sales and marketing to attract that new customer. Now protect your investment by turning the customer into a long-term asset.

Here are just a few questions that can help test your willingness to invest in customer retention. Would you or your company:

1. Hire customer service auditors to provide regular evaluations of your operations?
2. Enroll all new employees in a thorough orientation and training course before they are ever allowed to get near a customer?

3. Add a substantial crew of part-time phone-answering personnel to reduce long phone holds and busy signals?

4. Install a toll-free customer hotline, staffed (or voice-responsed) 24 hours a day, seven days a week?

5. Mail an annual thank-you letter to every customer, with a customer service survey included?

6. Pay bonuses to employees with exceptional customer service records?

7. Adopt a more liberal returned-goods or service-refund policy?

8. Offer premiums, awards, or other recognition to loyal, long-term customers?

Identify Customer Values; Set Standards; and Monitor Results

City Trust of New York determined what service values were most important to its customers, and highest on the list were timeliness, accuracy, and responsiveness. The company also identified key customer-interaction points such as handling a loan application. Then it set service standards, including such requirements as meeting with the customer within five days of the first contact and making a commitment within 30 days. Finally, City Trust set up a monitoring system to see that standards were being met. Currently, from 10 to 15 customer interviews are done daily to learn if people are getting the service they expect.

This sort of systematic research, standard setting, and monitoring is necessary if a company is to stay current with its customers' expectations. At Federal Express, supervisors monitor every customer phone agent according to a set of research-generated standards. For example, phone agents are expected to answer within three rings, speak clearly and pleasantly, and always remember to thank the customer. Depending upon what part of the country you're in, Federal Express phone agents are also selected partly on the basis of their regional accent because research showed this is one of the "values" that's important to customers in certain areas.

American Express, the credit card company, has what *Fortune* magazine says "may be the world's most elaborate system for tracking service quality." At American Express, continuous monitoring is done on more than 100 customer-interaction points, covering such standards as processing new cards within 15 days, replacing lost or stolen cards in one day, and sending out error-free bills. This kind of dedication to detail has earned the company a superior customer satisfaction rating and enabled it to charge premium fees both to its cardholders and the businesses that accept the cards.

Be Hungry for Customer Feedback

Feedback from customers is life-and-death sustenance to any service-oriented company, and when encouraged, most customers love to dish it out.

Encouragement is the most important ingredient. To get ample and useful feedback, companies have to invite it and make it convenient for the customer to respond.

There are many methods and tools for cultivating and gathering customer feedback. Below are some of the most commonly used and effective ones:

- Telephone surveys (always keep them short and call at convenient times)
- Mail surveys (again, make them short and enclose postage-prepaid envelopes)
- In-store suggestion boxes or kiosks (place where every customers passes by)
- Mystery shoppers who may chat with customers
- Focus groups (small, informal, and held in attractive, comfortable locations)
- Store or mall "intercept" interviews
- Interactive video devices

Don't Let Them Leave Without Finding Out Why

There are few people more brutally honest than angry ex-customers. They're ready to spill their stories in lurid detail to anyone who'll listen. But, like the jilted lover, the company is usually the last to know why the love affair ended.

Anytime you lose a customer, you should do whatever you can to find out why they've left. If it's at all feasible, a ranking executive or upper-middle manager should try to speak with the customer personally, either face-to-face or by phone. It might be an embarrassing experience, but you're more likely to get candid answers; and there's also the possibility that the customer might be impressed enough by the personal attention to give the company one more chance.

At the very least, departing customers should be sent a printed "exit-interview" form (with prepaid postage, naturally) and be asked politely to explain their experience with the company. A sample of such a form used by a bank is shown in Figures 3–1 and 3–2.

Respect and Use Your Employees' Ideas

Both frontline and backroom employees can be excellent sources of ideas on quality and service. But, like customers, they have to be encouraged to speak out and to be given a handy means of doing so.

At Globe Metallurgical, the CEO meets with all hourly employees every month to discuss quality. Meanwhile, hourly workers are paid overtime for their weekly "Quality Circle" meetings, which take place either before or after their regular shifts. Management adheres to a strict policy of addressing all employee suggestions and quality-related questions within 24 hours, and the door is always open to the CEO's office for employees who want to advance their ideas on quality or productivity.

FIGURE 3–1

Closed-Account Survey Letter

Closed-Account Survey

Dear Customer:

Our primary goal is to provide the best service possible. Therefore, we are always concerned when a customer closes an account.

We would like to know about your experience with us. Please take a few minutes to answer the questions on the enclosed form. Your answers will be completely confidential and will help us improve the quality of our service.

After completing the questionnaire, simply fold it and mail it back to us. No postage is required.

Thank you for your assistance. We value your comments and hope we may serve you again in the future.

Sincerely,

Chairman and
Chief Executive Officer

The Westinghouse Nuclear Fuels Division received 1,050 quality-improvement suggestions from its employees in 1988, and the company accepted and implemented 82 percent of those ideas.

Methods for stimulating and gathering employees' ideas will vary from one company to the next. What's important is to reach out to employees and then treat their thoughts with seriousness and respect.

Below is a sample "Employee Service Assessment Survey" (Figure 3–3) that might be used as a model to gather ideas in your own company. Following it is a sample questionnaire asking employees to help define "quality service" in their particular business (Figure 3–4).

FIGURE 3–2

Closed-Account Survey Form

---

1. How long have you been a customer with (company name)?

   _____

---

2. How long did you have the account that recently closed?

   ☐ Under 2 years   ☐ 2–4 years   ☐ 5 years or more

---

3. Please indicate the reason or reasons you closed this account:

   ☐ Moved away from the (city name) area

   ☐ Account was no longer needed

   ☐ Company made errors on account

   ☐ Service was slow or inefficient

   ☐ Personnel were discourteous or unfriendly

   ☐ Another (city name) area company is more convenient

   ☐ Account at another company meets my needs better

   ☐ Other (specify)_____

   _____

   _____

---

4. Where did you *replace* this account? (Please check only one)

   ☐ (Major competitor's name)

   ☐ A (city name) company

   ☐ Other (specify)_____

   ☐ Did not replace account

---

5. Which of our outlets did you use most often?

   _____

FIGURE 3–2

continued

---

6. Please fill in the blank that applies to you:

    I do most of my service with_____

    I have one or more accounts with_____
    but I do most of my service with another company.

    I no longer have any accounts with_____

---

7. How would you rate (company) in each of the following areas?

	Excellent	Average	Poor
Courteous and friendly personnel	☐	☐	☐
Knowledgeable personnel	☐	☐	☐
Prompt service	☐	☐	☐
Accurate statements	☐	☐	☐

---

8. Please indicate your age group:

    ☐ Under 25   ☐ 25–29   ☐ 30–44   ☐ 45–54   ☐ 55–64   ☐ 65+

---

9. Please indicate your annual household income category:

    ☐ Under $15,000   ☐ $15,999–24,999   ☐ $25,000–34,999
    ☐ $35,000–49,999   ☐ $50,000 or more

Any comments that will assist us in improving the quality of our service
or our products:_____
_____
_____
_____
_____

Thank you for your help,

_____
Chief Service Officer

FIGURE 3–3

Employee Assessment Survey Form

Employee Assessment Survey

We continually look for ways to improve service to our customers. Your ideas and suggestions will be a very important part of our plans to provide better service. Please complete this questionnaire and be candid about your observations. Because you have regular contact with our customers, you know best where improvement is needed.

Please return the questionnaire, unsigned, to (*name/department*) by (*date*). Thank you for your suggestions.

1. How do you feel our service compares with the service provided by (primary competitors)?
   _____
   _____
   _____

2. What problems do you face in delivering high-quality service to your customers?
   _____
   _____
   _____

3. Which one of the above is the greatest problem you face?
   _____
   _____
   _____

4. What feedback regarding service do you receive from your customers most frequently?
   _____
   _____
   _____

5. What changes would you make to improve service to your customers?
   _____
   _____
   _____

FIGURE 3–3

continued

6. What gets in the way of your delivering good service?

_____

_____

_____

7. Why do you think customers leave?

_____

_____

_____

Thank you for your help,

_____

Chief Service Officer

Be Consistent

Although all customers are individuals with their own personal tastes and attitudes, they nonetheless appreciate consistency in service. There are comfort and confidence levels associated with knowing that you'll get the same treatment and value for your money every time you go to a particular store, restaurant, or hotel, or every time you fly a particular airline.

McDonald's is an outstanding example of a company that has mastered consistency. You get the same Big Mac delivered in the same way whether you're in Baltimore or Istanbul.

When Kemmons Wilson founded Holiday Inns, his central purpose and strategy were to offer a consistent lodging package for American families on the road. In fact, the very idea for Holiday Inns came to him while he was on

FIGURE 3–4

Sample "Quality Service" Questionnaire for Employees

Sample Employee Questionnaire: Developing a Definition of Quality

In our continuing efforts to improve service quality, we will attempt to define what "quality of service" means to (institution name). This definition will become the foundation for our service quality program.

Your opinions are important! Please complete this brief questionnaire and return it, unsigned, to (name/department) by (date).

1. Which of the following are important elements in your definition of quality service?

	Important Part of Quality Definition	Not an Important Part of Quality Definition
Promptness of service	☐	☐
Professionalism of staff	☐	☐
Accuracy of information	☐	☐
Clarity of statements/billings	☐	☐
Courtesy of staff	☐	☐
Knowledge of staff	☐	☐
Reputation of company	☐	☐
Friendliness of staff	☐	☐
Availability of brochures/information	☐	☐
Hours of operation	☐	☐
Other_____	☐	☐

2. If you were responsible for developing a written definition of quality for (name), what definition would you recommend?

FIGURE 3–4

continued

3. In your opinion, what should the standards of quality be for
    each of the following?

    During Peak Times:
    Answer telephone   _____ rings
    Wait in line   _____ minutes
    Respond to complaint   _____ days
    Wait for service delivery   _____ days

a long motoring trip with his family in the 1950s. He was
appalled at the unpleasant surprises he confronted with
each stop at a locally owned independent motel.

Not every business has to be a chain or franchise organization in order to achieve service consistency. Even the
family-owned restaurant that's noted for its unique cui-
sine or atmosphere is expected to offer a known, reliable
level of service and value every time you dine there. But
it takes planning and continual monitoring to maintain
such levels. The service at too many restaurants varies
daily or at different times of day according to which cooks
and waiters are on duty; and this happens because owners or managers have not established firm standards and
are not continuously measuring results.

There's an old management saying: "If it doesn't get
measured, it doesn't get done." It's equally valid to say
that if you don't measure what's going on today, you have
no way of setting standards for consistency in the future.

Following are two examples of yardsticks for measuring
service consistency—one for internal use at a bank (Figure
3–5) and the other for surveying passengers of an airline
(Figure 3–6).

FIGURE 3–5

Bank Service Consistency Checklist

	Always	Sometimes	Never
I. Officer quality			
• Do our customers perceive officers to be experienced and knowledgeable?	( )	( )	( )
• Do our customers think we understand their business?	( )	( )	( )
• Do our customers think our account officers have the authority to make decisions?	( )	( )	( )
II. Officer turnover			
• Do we handle the transition of account officer to our customers' satisfaction?	( )	( )	( )
III. Responsiveness			
• Do we respond to loan requests in a timely fashion?	( )	( )	( )
• Do we handle resolutions of problems thoroughly and in a timely manner?	( )	( )	( )
IV. Recognition of customer			
• Do we consistently recognize customer business?	( )	( )	( )
• Are our customers recognized in branches?	( )	( )	( )
• Do our customers get the attention they want from top executive management?	( )	( )	( )
Total	☐	☐	☐

FIGURE 3–6

In-Flight Quality Assurance Form

Y = Yes	N = No	N/A = Not Applicable	
[Y]	[N]	[N/A]	Were you greeted in a friendly manner?
[Y]	[N]	[N/A]	Were you directed to your seat?
[Y]	[N]	[N/A]	Was there an offer to hang your coat?(FC)
[Y]	[N]	[N/A]	Was flt/dest announcement made prior to door closing?
[Y]	[N]	[N/A]	Smoking regulations announced?
[Y]	[N]	[N/A]	Frequent flight bonus announcement?
[Y]	[N]	[N/A]	If flight delayed, were passengers informed?
[Y]	[N]	[N/A]	Announcements clear and professional?
[Y]	[N]	[N/A]	Safety demo professional?
[Y]	[N]	[N/A]	Were magazines distributed?
[Y]	[N]	[N/A]	Were drink orders taken (F only)?
[Y]	[N]	[N/A]	Were passengers names used (F only)?
[Y]	[N]	[N/A]	Did the service appear organized?
[Y]	[N]	[N/A]	Were entree orders taken (F only)?
[Y]	[N]	[N/A]	Meals/beverages served in a timely way?
[Y]	[N]	[N/A]	Did meal appear appetizing?
[Y]	[N]	[N/A]	Was meal the correct temperature?

FIGURE 3–6

continued

[Y]	[N]	[N/A]	Did you enjoy the meal?
[Y]	[N]	[N/A]	Dishes/trays removed in a timely way?
[Y]	[N]	[N/A]	Name tags on serving garments?
[Y]	[N]	[N/A]	Connection gates given?
[Y]	[N]	[N/A]	Were you thanked for your business?
[Y]	[N]	[N/A]	After meal service, was F/A visible?
[Y]	[N]	[N/A]	Were flight attendants well-groomed?
[Y]	[N]	[N/A]	Were flight attendants warm and friendly?
[Y]	[N]	[N/A]	Were flight attendants professional?

Rate the overall inflight service 1–5
1 2 3 4 5

Know Your Competition and How You Compare

There are plenty of ways to gather intelligence about your competitors—and no excuse not to do so. Yet many managers carry false assumptions about how they stack up against the competition, either because they haven't gathered the proper intelligence or they've gotten it and misread its real significance.

One of the worst mistakes is to become complacent because you find that your own service is no worse than the competition's. A sharp competitor may be ready to jump out front with a new service program while you're left standing in the exhaust. If you're just about even, why not take the initiative yourself? There are customers out there for the taking if you offer them something better.

In today's increasingly conglomerated economy, you may have competitors that you're not yet aware of or some who are just about ready to move in on your market. The banking field is a good example. First National may be no better or worse than Last National, but there are other companies from totally different industries now offering traditional or alternative banking services—companies such as Sears, Merrill Lynch, GMAC, and Ford Motor Credit. It's getting tougher to tell who the players are and who the new ones might be tomorrow or next week. And as new ones enter the game, they bring skills with them that you may find unfamiliar. To be a winner, you have to continually look into the other team's huddle.

Figure 3–7 presents a "Competitive Analysis Worksheet" that suggests ways in which you might compare your service offering to that of your competition.

The Closer to the Customer, the Better

Management needs to stay in closer touch with customers. There are often too many buffer zones of supervisors and lower-level managers who shut key decisionmakers off from the day-to-day customer action. Executives also hide from customer contact by investing most of their time in "more important" matters such as committee meetings, conferences, and reviewing stacks of documents and reports whose value may be questionable. And lately, a disproportionate share of management time and talent has been diverted to the high-stakes but service-blind games of corporate takeovers and mergers.

At the levels of management where customer interests can be given the most clout, customers are usually the last and least important subject of concern. Yet they are the people who actually pay the bills for everything else,

FIGURE 3–7

Competitive Analysis Worksheet

Competitive Analysis Worksheet

Facts You Need to Know

Competitor's name _____

Total resources $ _____ Outlets _____

Corporate goals: _____
_____
_____

Target market segments: _____
_____
_____

Product offering/product line compared to us: _____
_____
_____

Product strategy: _____
_____
_____

Promotion strategy/typical means of promotion: _____
_____
_____

Assessment of promotion effectiveness: _____
_____
_____

Relative product and service quality compared to us: _____
_____
_____

Location/distribution compared to us: _____
_____
_____

FIGURE 3–7

continued

Consumer perception/image in the marketplace: _____

_____

_____

Strengths: _____

_____

_____

Key market advantage: _____

_____

_____

Weaknesses: _____

_____

_____

Key market disadvantage: _____

_____

_____

Overall assessment of competitor's impact on us: _____

_____

_____

---

and their interests should come much higher on the list of priorities.

It isn't enough, however, for top management to tack customer service on the agenda as a postscript or side issue to the latest budget report or merger strategy. Managers must take the time to actually rub elbows with customers and frontline employees.

Motorola chairman Robert Galvin visits customers regularly. As he explains, "I stay away from the big shots, though. When I go to a customer's plant, I spend my time with the engineers, expediters, supervisors, and line workers—and I ask them, 'what can we do to improve our quality and service?'" Galvin began these regular visits in 1984 and went to 12 customer locations that year. Now he tries to visit twice that many, and *all* of Motorola's senior executives and unit managers are *required* to make frequent customer visits.

Avoid Exaggerated Promises

When a company loudly proclaims, "We do it *all* for you," and then something goes wrong, customers become even more cynical. If the company can actually live up to its advertised promise of 100-percent satisfaction, then it's all right to publicize the fact; except that in most cases, it *isn't* a fact—not even in the best-run, most service-conscious companies.

It's smarter to invest in things that can improve service—things like better training, higher wages, and technology—and then let the results speak for themselves through word-of-mouth customer endorsements.

Stay Away from Gimmicks

Many companies dabble in sporadic or one-shot efforts to improve service. They provide a training course here, a mystery shopper there, a once-a-year survey, an occasional employee award, a year-of-the-customer campaign, or bumperstickers that say "thank-you-for-shopping-at-our-store."

However, gimmicks are usually worse than no effort at all. They create a false sense of security and even smugness among managers. They also tend to draw attention away from glaring faults in service delivery, while obscuring the point that consistently good customer service requires substantial resources and a full-time, ongoing commitment.

Customers, who are getting more and more sophisticated, see through most gimmicks and are unimpressed. And

employees are often embarrassed by the outright buffoon-
ery of such tricks.

Low Prices Don't Always Beat Good Service

Pricing is an important competitive strategy. Many companies use it episodically to attract new customers or
rebuild sagging volume. Others, such as discount stores
and warehouse outlets, rely on low price as their central
appeal. But, in the words of Stanley Marcus, "Long after
the thrill of the low price is gone, the reality of *quality*
remains."

The best price bargain can sour in the face of poor quality or bad service. Customers will consciously make trade-
offs, as they do when they patronize self-serve, no-frills
discount stores. Sometimes you go to a fast-food outlet for
a $1.25 hamburger, but you *know* what you're supposed
to get for your $1.25; and you've already agreed to forego
certain service amenities. Other times, you want to go to
a fine restaurant and be served a $22.50 filet mignon with
all the trimmings and trappings that are supposed to justify the price. In both cases, however, your expectations
have to be met. The hamburger has to be cooked right,
served on a fresh bun, and delivered to you by a clerk
with clean hands and a freshly laundered uniform. The
filet mignon has to be high quality, done to your taste,
and served on good china by an attentive waiter.

No matter what a company's pricing strategy may be,
there is *always* an implicit, if not explicit, service level
that customers associate with the price level. Bargain-
basement prices don't mean that customers will totally
ignore such things as long waiting lines, rude personnel, dirty surroundings, or defective products. With all
the options available today, customers can almost always
go to a competitor who offers similar prices but better
service. And many times, they will even pay more for
the same product. A consumer survey by the daily trade
paper *American Banker* showed that people switch banks

because of poor service, *not* because of lower fees or better interest rates elsewhere.

The same kind of thinking is becoming more prevalent among quality-conscious manufacturers. Kenneth Leach of Globe Metallurgical says that his company neither sells nor buys primarily on the basis of price. "We're able to charge a good price for our products," says Leach, "because they're of superior quality, and our customers can't afford to buy something less than that. By the same token, we don't bargain hunt when we buy raw materials because if we're going to turn out top quality, we have to start with the best ingredients."

Customers Buy Benefits, Not Products or Services

In the earliest days of the automobile era, Henry Ford said he wasn't in the business of building cars but of "providing transportation for people." Detroit forgot that basic premise for the next 70 years, until the Ford Motor Company rediscovered it in the 1980s and declared once again that it doesn't build cars but "creates driver and passenger satisfaction."

Every company must remember this: customers don't pay for a physical product or delivered service; they pay for the *utility* or *satisfaction* it will give them. Perfume manufacturers and marketers don't sell little bottles of chemicals and exotic plant juices; they sell romance, intrigue, and self-confidence. Bankers are not in the banking business; they're in the business of helping people protect their money and making it grow. And watchmakers don't make watches; they make it possible for people to know what time it is.

Too many businesses have lost this all-important perspective on what it is they actually do to stay in business and make money. Managers and employees become fixated on the product or delivered service, forgetting the customer's real purpose for being there.

Customer Loyalty Has to Be Earned Over and Over Again

Most customers would like to be loyal to a company that offers a good product, reasonable price, and convenience in buying. But their loyalty has to be reciprocated. The company must recognize the customer and show that it appreciates the business.

There are many ways in which a company can earn and return a customer's loyalty. Examples include special sale events for frequent shoppers, earned discount points, airline frequent-flyer programs, and special room rates for regular or frequent hotel guests. But loyalty doesn't always have to be rewarded strictly in economic terms. Customers also value personal attention, assistance in solving problems, and a sense of security and confidence that a company can give them. Simple thank-you notes and greeting cards often go a long way toward making a customer feel appreciated. And a phone call to check on the customer's satisfaction after a major purchase can be very effective.

It's important, too, that a company pay attention to the steady but *small* customers. Big-spenders are often wined and dined, taken on fishing or skiing trips, or invited to play golf. Smaller customers rarely if ever get treated so royally. But a company can score big points by occasionally doing something special for the little customer. For example, an elderly couple might have bought from you in small amounts for the last 10 or 15 years, and it wouldn't hurt for a manager to invite them to lunch. The word-of-mouth public relations value of such efforts is generally overlooked.

High Tech Can't Replace the Personal Touch

Remember that the more automated a company gets, the greater the tendency will be to leave the customer's fate in the hands of the machines.

Automation and computers are wonderful tools. But no matter how often we use the high-tech buzzword "user-friendly," the fact is that no machine or electronic system is capable of real human friendliness.

Let the machines do the jobs they were designed to do, but don't expect them to "interface" with customers with the personal touch that only you and your employees are capable of.

Don't Run Your Business Like a Police State

Nobody wants to be an easy mark for thieves, and every company needs reasonable security to prevent cheating by customers. But security is one thing, and paranoia is another. Companies should always consider customers innocent unless proven guilty. The law requires this, and so does common sense. If you suspect that every merchandise return or refund request is fraudulent, you will undoubtedly expose the ones that actually are. But what about the ones that are legitimate? By putting every unhappy customer through a grilling, you will automatically alienate those who have valid complaints. In the long run, this will be more costly than having a few real thieves slip through your dragnet.

The same philosophy applies to late-payment notices. Avoid using an accusatory or threatening tone because the customer actually may not be at fault; you might end up alienating a loyal customer who had an unavoidable problem during the billing period in question. The *real* deadbeats won't respond to dunning notices anyway, regardless of how such notices are worded. Once you know that you've got a hard case on your hands, let your collection agency or legal department take it from there.

An overly authoritarian, imperious, or suspicious management style can also wreck employee morale. Never embarrass or put any employee on the spot in front of customers or other employees. If real discipline is needed, take the employee behind closed doors to discuss the problem, and unless you have concrete knowledge that an employee has done something dishonest or patently irresponsible, remember the he or she is still innocent until proven otherwise. This not only makes good management sense; it could also save you costly legal problems.

Take Care of the Details

Big impressions are formed from small experiences— sometimes from an accumulation of little things and other times from a single event. The rental car, for example, might be fine in every regard except that one windshield-wiper blade needs replacing. The restaurant food may be appetizing and reasonably priced, but the waiter is always looking in another direction when you want to get his attention. Taken alone, these are small matters, but they can color your total impression of the car rental agency and restaurant.

Many managers think they are too busy or their jobs are too important for them to worry about whether the floor is clean, the restrooms have enough tissue, or the phones are getting answered promptly. Conversely, frontline employees may think their jobs are too limited in scope for them to worry about such matters. They're getting paid to do a specific job, and that's all they care to do.

The problem is that, although neither managers nor employees are looking at these details, customers are seeing them very clearly and forming a broad impression of the company. Sooner or later, it will take just one more mishandled detail to drive the customer away.

Build Better Supplier Relationships

Diners and hotel guests don't blame the linen-supply company when they get dirty napkins and towels. They may not realize the linen-supply company even exists; they simply blame the restaurant or hotel. If an axle or spring on a new car breaks, the once-proud owner of that car will blame the automaker—not the steel company that poured low-quality steel or the fabricator that shaped the spring.

Every business is dependent upon suppliers, and no total-quality effort can succeed unless suppliers are carefully selected and brought into the program as valued resources who have an important stake in your success.

A vital part of the Ford turnaround was the company's revolutionary restructuring of its supplier relationships. Like the other American automakers, Ford traditionally had bought components from a great many suppliers, with price as the main determinant. Quality suffered under this arrangement because suppliers were always under pressure to cut costs whatever the results; and with the same types of components coming from so many different sources, there was inconsistency in product standards. Ford decided to buy from far fewer suppliers—those who were willing and able to work more closely with the company on quality assurance and just-in-time delivery. The automaker also earnestly solicited suppliers' ideas on ways to improve components, manufacturing processes, and the final product—Ford cars and trucks. Suppliers who could and would measure up to the new standards were rewarded with ongoing contracts for larger volumes of business, and this, in turn, enabled them to make their own operations more cost-effective and profitable. These suppliers today are designated by Ford as "Q-1 Preferred Suppliers" with the "Q-1" reflecting the Ford slogan, "Quality is Job One."

Other manufacturers engaged in serious quality-improvement programs have built similar supplier networks in recent years. General Motors issues its "Mark of Excellence" awards to high-performance suppliers. The Xerox Corporation has narrowed its supplier base from more than 2,500 to a select group of 350. Westinghouse says its goal is "to make our suppliers valued business partners with primary emphasis on high quality and on-time delivery." Robert Galvin of Motorola says that all of his company's suppliers *must* make a commitment to apply for the Baldrige National Quality Award at some point in the foreseeable future. Not all of them will win the award, of course, but the very act of completing the application forces a company to closely examine itself and face up to the quality challenge. Even tiny Globe Metallurgical has a formal supplier program. Globe trains its suppliers in how to meet the company's standards, audits their performance annually, and grants Globe certification to "preferred" suppliers.

Whether you do business as a manufacturer, fast-food operator, hotel, or florist shop, the way you select and work with your suppliers can make or break any effort to improve your delivery of customer satisfaction. Find out who your best or most promising suppliers are, and then work out a partnership with them to your mutual advantage. Insist on high quality and reliable service, show them how they can meet your requirements better, ask their advice, and be willing to reward them with continuing business at a fair price.

Always Keep Thinking about What Customers Want

Customer want-lists vary from one type of business to another; and even within the same business, the relative importance of certain customer needs and wants will fluctuate from time to time. There are, however, some constants that apply just about all the time in any kind of business. Although they seem to be self-evident, it's important that managers keep customer wants in mind:

1. Promptness (never having to wait for service)
2. Professionalism (confidence in the company's knowledge and character)
3. Accuracy (confidence that things will be done right)
4. Personal treatment (not becoming a statistic)

5. Courtesy (friendliness, respect, trust)
7. Product or service fulfillment (quality & reliability)
8. Willingness to listen (the customer wants to be heard)
9. Price/value legitimacy (getting what you pay for)
10. Acceptable physical facilities (accessible, clean, and safe)

Know the Cost of Losing a Customer

Most businesses know what it costs them to get a new customer, but few know that it costs to lose an existing one. Losing a customer usually has a "domino effect," which is poorly understood or not recognized at all by management.

Below are two sample techniques for calculating the real cost when a customer leaves (Tables 3–1 and 3–2).

TABLE 3–1

*Sample Financial Impact of Lost Customers
(department store)*

Accounts lost:	1,000 accounts
	×$ 1,500 average annual revenue
	$1,500,000
Profit lost:	$1,500,000 lost annual revenue
	× .15 profit margin
	$ 225,000 profit lost
Account closing costs:	$ 10 estimated cost to close account
	× 1,000
	$ 10,000 administration costs
	$225,000 profit lost
	+$ 10,000 admin cost
	$235,000 bottom line cost

TABLE 3–2

Marketing Cost of Lost Customers (general example)

Estimated marketing cost per customer	$250
Average monthly turnover of customers	150 customers
Marketing dollars lost as the result of turnover of customers (50% of original investment)	$18,750 per month
Lost revenue from 150 customers at $25 per month	$3,750 per month
Cost to attract 150 new customers	$37,500
Total cost to lose and replace 150 customers	$60,000

Honestly Assess Your Customer-Service Commitment

Senior executives need to be completely candid with themselves and their colleagues in determining just how good or bad their company's customer service levels are. To do this, it's helpful to put the question and answers on paper in a formal, systematic way. Following is a sample format for evaluating your commitment to customer service.

FIGURE 3–8

Test Your Customer Satisfaction Service Commitment

Question	Yes	No
Does your company/do you:		
1. Have a mission- or vision-statement that includes customer service?		
2. Have image/position in the marketplace that includes customer service (i.e., expect excellence, "absolutely, positively overnight")?		
3. Conduct regular ongoing customer service surveys?		
4. Set standards for each customer service contact point?		
5. Audit service levels?		
6. Track why customers start/stop using your products or services and provide easy access for customers to voice complaints?		
7. Regularly thank customers for their business? Regularly evaluate customer complaints?		
8. Communicate to all employees through meetings, speeches, or newsletters the importance of customer satisfaction?		
9. Know the total cost of acquiring a new customer and the cost of losing a customer?		
10. Provide ongoing customer service training?		
11. Include customer service bonuses or incentives as part of your compensation program?		
12. Have a quality-improvement process to provide error-free service?		
Total		

KEY TO FIGURE 3–8

Score on Service Commitment Test

Yes Answers	
10–12	Customer satisfaction STAR. Your company has probably received recognition for its service levels— a rare achievement for an American company. Apply for the National Quality Award.
7–9	Customer satisfaction in sight. Not there yet, but something is starting to happen. Moved from vision to making it reality.
3–6	Inconsistent at best. Sometimes it's good; sometimes it's bad. Neither employees nor customers are getting a clear message.
0–2	Customer service is mostly lip service.

4

DAY-TO-DAY
SERVICE
MANAGEMENT

CUSTOMER DISCONTENT most often arises immediately following a purchase, and it's usually related either to employee apathy or a lack of authority for the employee to correct the problem on the spot.

One company that does an exceptional job of dealing with these roadblocks is Nordstrom, Inc., a specialty department store company that began as a family shoe business in 1901 at Seattle, Washington. Nordstrom today has 41 department stores and 15 specialty operations concentrated on the West Coast but with new stores opening up in Virginia, Maryland, and New Jersey. In spite of its growth into a far-flung organization employing more than 20,000 people, the company is still managed much like a "friendly neighborhood business," where the customer comes first and employees are motivated and rewarded to provide outstanding service. Nordstrom's operates by these maxims: *Listen to the customer; the customer is always right; and do anything to satisfy the customer.* Management actually lives up to those principles, and the results are not only happy, loyal customers, but also service-conscious, loyal employees. As one retailing analyst put it, "Nordstrom has no problem attracting the cream of the crop to work for it. People like to work for a winner, and people like to be appreciated by their employers."

Nordstrom's general policy is to always accept returned merchandise, with no questions asked, and *every* salesperson has full authority to take back the returned goods without having to get a supervisor's approval or do complicated paperwork. In fact, employees are technically required to accept the goods and make the refund or exchange, but, in those few cases of clearly evident customer fraud, the salesperson also has the authority to make an exception to the policy. Interestingly, it is only these rare exceptions that require filing a report. And lest Nordstrom be mistaken for a real pushover, it should be noted that the company does have a fairly sophisticated tracking system that red-flags flagrant customer scams. If a customer makes a habit of returning clothing items on Mondays following special weekend events, Nordstrom eventually puts a stop to it. The company is occasionally victimized by people who take advantage of its liberal returned-goods policy, but management is convinced— and the record shows—that the good will, repeat business, and word-of-mouth promotional benefits far outweigh these losses. Furthermore, employees' workdays are more pleasant and productive because the employees are virtually never put on the defensive or required to haggle with a customer. Time goes faster and people are more relaxed in their jobs if they can simply say, "That's no problem. We'll take care of that for you right away."

This strategy works at Nordstrom because frontline employees are given a clear statement of company policy and are then allowed the freedom and the respect for their own judgment; they carry out that policy without having to be second-guessed or to go through a tiresome bureaucratic procedure. Well-screened before hiring and well-trained afterwards, Nordstrom employees are treated as intelligent adults, and when they perform as expected, they are nicely rewarded with bonuses and other extras.

Each month, Nordstrom stores hold sales rallies involving all department managers and any employees who are to be singled out for exemplary service. These rallies are always led by a high-ranking executive, including in many cases a member of the Nordstrom family. At one such rally attended by the author at the company's Seattle flagship store, co-chairman Bruce Nordstrom personally handed out cash bonuses to deserving employees. One employee got a $100 bonus because she had used part of her day off to make a two-hour round-trip bus journey across town to deliver a sweater to an elderly customer. Others receiving cash rewards included an employee who had gotten the most customer compliments for the month, another who had the most sales, and one who had made the most "extracurricular" customer contacts by phone and mail. Bruce and another family member, John Nordstrom, read aloud a large sampling of customer letters containing both compliments and complaints. And when the rally was over, all company personnel walked the stairs (five floors) in order to avoid clogging the elevators used by customers.

Another retailing company, L. L. Bean, pursues customer retention with a similar zeal. L. L. Bean managers are explicitly instructed to do whatever is necessary to satisfy an unhappy customer or bring a departing customer back into the fold. Since the company's merchandise is shipped to individual customers in very corner of the country, it would be normal to expect at least occasional slip-ups—the wrong merchandise being sent, late delivery, goods damaged in shipment, incorrect billings, and so on. But there are very few such breakdowns because the company's order-filling system is tightly geared to avoiding them. Employees are so thoroughly schooled in both the philosophy and the practical methods of customer-oriented service delivery, in those few cases where disappointed customers simply won't be mollified, the company internally circulates a form that says, "L. L. Bean lost a sale today," and the employees are asked to fill in the reason. To some, this may seem like a small, even irksome, exercise; but it is just such methods as these that are needed to continuously reinforce a customer satisfaction mindset among employees and managers. It's one of those small details that are building blocks for the bigger structure.

Lasting and effective customer retention programs such as those at Nordstrom and L. L. Bean begin with a true understanding of the sweeping and sustained commitment required at all levels of the organization. Managers at companies that are just beginning to emphasize quality or launch major service-improvement programs also need the courage to really shake up the organization and reshape it into a holistic system, in which all the necessary resources are applied in concert with one another.

A holistic entity is, by definition, "greater than the sum of its parts." It has an existence of its own, but that existence is altered or threatened if any one of the parts breaks down or becomes unsynchronized with the others. While the term "holistic" originated in the field of philosophy and has recently come to be associated with the field of medicine, it is also appropriate for describing the way in which companies of any size and type need to be organized.

Ford took a holistic approach to restoring its product quality. When the new management team began mapping the company's recovery strategy, they realized that Ford, like so many other U.S. corporations, was a fragmented organization with many of its parts working at cross purposes. Over the next five years, in preparing to launch its new family of cars that began with the 1986 Taurus, Ford rallied all of the people who had a contribution to make and began bringing previously isolated people together at the earliest stages of planning. People started thinking less about their own egos, job specialties, and short-term interests and began concentrating on what the company was trying to achieve as a whole. Alton F. Doody and Ron Bingaman, in their book *Reinventing the Wheels: Ford's Spectacular Comeback* (Ballinger, 1988), described the recovery this way:

No Lone Rangers would be riding to the rescue at Ford. The "hero" would be a *product,* not a person, and the success of that product would be attributable to and shared by everybody who had anything to do with it. Eventually, even the office and shop rhetoric would change. From an "I" company, Ford would become a "we" company. People started saying "we," "us," and "our" instead of "I," "me," and "mine." This change was not merely cosmetic, and it reflected something far more than a new etiquette or protocol. What was really happening at Ford was a transformation of the *corporate culture.* People were actually changing the way they viewed the company and how they interpreted their roles within it.

Meanwhile, even Ford's definition of its product would change. The company was no longer in the business of "building cars" but of "creating driver and passenger satisfaction." In fact, the introduction of the Taurus was delayed for some nine months because research kept uncovering more ways to improve upon that satisfaction. This delay cost the company millions of dollars in lost sales, but Ford was intent upon getting the cars right. As one executive put it at the time, "If anybody should 'eat' a problem, it should be *us* not our customer."

This attitude contrasts sharply with what we hear so often: "If they don't like it, they can go somewhere else. Who needs the headache?"

How does all this relate to the day-to-day management of service and the continuous creation of customer satisfaction? It relates because real improvement in service delivery cannot be achieved in most companies without a transformation of the corporate culture.

Traditional management roles are outmoded for the necessary focus on customer retention. Historically, American business schools have taught a top-down, hierarchical style of management, with heavy emphasis on control. But that strategy is changing. James Houghton of Corning believes that senior executives should exercise command on the big decisions and provide inspiration and vision. But he adds that ongoing operations should be organized "horizontally rather than vertically" and that, when things go right, "credit must be distributed throughout the group." More and more top executives realize that managing effectively means less top-down control are more horizontal exchange of ideas and supportive actions.

Once a person reaches the executive suite or the supervisor's office, he or she must work harder at being sensitive to what goes on at the employee-customer contact level. Concern for the customer must also be communicated constantly to the people in the ranks, and managers have to match their words with a real commitment of their own. Unless there is consistency between what management says is important and what is actually tallies on the scorecard, there will be a loss of credibility. You may attach the word "priority" to anything you choose, but if you don't follow up and *treat* it as such, you're not likely to be taken seriously.

Before priorities can be rearranged, senior executives need to take stock of just where they and their companies stand on service delivery and customer satisfaction. Everybody holds assumptions about their service levels, but a few hard questions, honestly answered, can poke holes in some of those assumptions. For example:

1. Do you know on a regular reporting basis how many customers you are losing?

2. Do you know how your company compares with the competition in getting and keeping customers?

3. Do you know where your company's delivery-chain problems occur?

4. Do you honestly want to hear the *truth* about customer service delivery and retention problems?

5. Do you require that your staff tell you the real costs of customer turnover?

6. Do you make customer retention an important theme in your management meetings?

7. Do you interact directly and frequently with people at all levels in your organization, and do you discuss customer retention with them?

8. Do you try to spend a significant amount of your time talking with customers of all types (happy ones, unhappy ones, and even ex-customers)?

9. Do you provide employees with incentives, rewards, and recognition for keeping customers?

10. Does your company have a policy of continuous improvement in customer service?

11. Do you commit significant resources to keeping customers as well as to getting customers?

If top management can answer yes to all or most of these questions, then the next areas of concern are middle and lower management.

Regardless of the type of company, middle managers and supervisors can act either as funnels or bottlenecks in service delivery. Even the best-intentioned, best-articulated service philosophies and policies coming out of boardrooms and executive suites can be slowed to a trickle or completely clogged by middle and lower management before they reach the customer-contact level. Conversely, middle and lower management can pump real life into the broad and sometimes grandly or blandly worded mission statements issued from the top. "The customer is king" rings meaningless unless managers translate those words into deeds.

While every company offers different opportunities for middle and lower management to take specific actions that can enhance service, there are certain fundamentals which apply in almost all types of businesses. In Chapter 2, we noted that one of the chief barriers to good service is the differences in people. Every manager has his or her unique crew of employees, who respond in their own distinct ways to different kinds of appeals, motivations, and requirements. In spite of these differences, there are basic responsibilities and actions required of middle and lower management to help create and maintain a customer-retention climate. Here are a selected few:

1. Listen closely to frontline employees to find out specifically what they need in order to do their jobs right.

2. Encourage employees to report problems and offer ideas for improvement.

3. See that the necessary tools and resources are provided to frontline employees.

4. Ensure that all job descriptions include customer orientation, and specify the impact that each person's job can have on customer retention.

5. Push decision-making authority down as far as possible, thereby allowing those with direct customer contact to do whatever is necessary to keep a customer.

6. Mediate or arbitrate disputes between departments or other managers to ensure that in-fighting doesn't affect customers.

7. Develop interdepartmental retention-improvement teams and problem-prevention groups.

8. Coordinate with other departments and staff functions to focus all available resources on ways of keeping customers.

9. Continuously monitor service levels.

10. Measure customer loss and pinpoint the exact reasons why any customer leaves.

In most companies, especially larger ones, middle and lower managers are usually segregated departmentally or according to technical or professional specialty. Ford chairman Donald Petersen described this organizational scheme at the "old" Ford Motor Company as a series of "chimneys," with each management group isolated in a self-contained vertical enclosure, unable or unwilling to communicate with counterparts in the other chimneys.

If a company is to get the most out of all its resources, these chimney-like structures have to be broken down or not allowed to rise in the first place. Personnel, operations, finance, research, marketing—all of these as well as others have their own unique tools, talents, and information pools to contribute to the common goal of keeping customers. But they have to talk with one another, and they each have to accept their share of the task.

Let's examine a few of the ways in which these specialized groups can do more to aid the cause.

Finance Department

Finance people are in a good position to quantify what it costs to acquire a new customer and to lose an existing one.

In the first case—customer acquisition—many finance departments are already up to speed. There are well-developed systems for tracking and measuring marketing, promotion, and selling costs as well as the setup costs for operations to get a new customer into the system. There are also ways of averaging these costs out on a customer-by-customer basis so that management can say, "It costs us 'X' dollars for every new customer we get."

In the second case—the cost of losing a customer— finance people typically are on unfamiliar ground, and they as well as senior management need to begin thinking in new terms. For instance, what kinds of equations are needed to determine the break-even point in the lifetime of a customer relationship? How do you know when the cost of acquiring a customer has been amortized and the company is making a profit from the acquisition? The markup or profit margin on the original sale does not necessarily answer this question, even though some sort of average attrition cost might have been factored into the price. In the cable television business, for example, customers who pay extra for Showtime or Home Box Office continue using those services for an average of 13 months.

The question arises: At what point during those 13 months does the company go in the black—not merely for a single customer, but for the market segment, or niche, as a whole? In other words, what is the dollar value to the cable company over the average lifetime of a Showtime or Home Box Office subscription, what is the cost of losing a subscriber before the "normal" 13-month period is up, and how can that loss be prevented?

For every company which depends on repeat sales or prolonged customer relationships, the loss of a customer has a ripple effect. Beyond the immediate loss of a sale, and aside from damage to the company's reputation, there are "hidden" costs that many companies fail to track. Yet the tracking shouldn't be difficult because there is almost always a trail of work associated with serving that customer. There are records of refunds, error resolutions, repair service, transaction-processing costs, and even the clerical and management time expended in dealing with the customer. What's missing now is the customer; what's left is a history of effort that is no longer paying off; and what's needed is a way to quantify that effort in dollar terms so that management can understand the cost/benefit tradeoff of keeping or losing a customer.

Finance departments can also help resolve other basic issues related to customer loss. For example, does the company's budgeting process have built-in assumptions that poor service and customer loss are "normal" features of doing business, or is the cost of losing customers treated as a controllable variable? Should there be an "acceptable" loss level, or should a section of the budget reflect the true cost of customer turnover? How budgeting is done reflects the way in which a company views its customers. In companies that have finely honed quality-improvement programs, costs are broken into such categories as problem prevention, detection, inspection, repairs, and other activities related to the cost of keeping customers.

Some industries are beginning to calculate the lifetime value of a customer. Ford knows that over a lifetime, a customer could buy more than $100,000 worth of auto-mobiles; thus, it makes no sense to alienate a customer over one small event. Likewise, the supermarket industry figures a customer will buy more than $250,000 worth of groceries in a lifetime, so the question of refunding a $5 item takes on a different perspective.

Operations

Depending upon the type of business or the individual company, "operations" may be called something else. It may come under a different group title, or there may be no distinct group at all that has the full range of activities we normally think of as "store operations" or "plant oper-ations." Those activities may be divided up among several groups. Whatever the nomenclature, in most companies there is an umbrella-like set of functions that keep the firm operating on a day-to-day basis. These may include managing physical facilities, scheduling business hours, assigning staff, managing paperflow and computer sys-tems, and coordinating the activities of all the other spe-cialized departments. What is so often ignored or under-emphasized, however, is the responsibility that operations managers should have for service delivery and customer satisfaction.

In the delivery of a product or service, there is a chain of events cutting across departmental boundaries, which needs to be diagrammed and continuously inspected to ensure that all its links are in place. Someone should have an overview of how the chain fits together and be in a position to predict where breaks may occur. The question arises: At what junctures is it most likely that a customer can become dissatisfied? The scene at almost any bank on a Friday afternoon is a good example. There stand the lines of frustrated customers who got to the lobby just before it closed, and outside are the lines of cars leading to the drive-up windows. It's true that most banks in recent years have abandoned the traditional "bankers' hours" and are offering customers alternative ways of doing business such as banking-by-mail and 24-hour automated teller machines. But there are many banking transactions that people don't want to make by machine or through the mail, and long bank lines on Friday afternoons are a too familiar aggravation. What the banks in these cases fail to recognize or refuse to accept is their own responsibility for repairing this weak link in their service chain. With those same Friday afternoon scenes recurring week in and week out, year after year, it's about time somebody in the banks said, "*We've* got a service problem. All those customers can't simply be procrastinators all the time. They must be trying to tell us something."

A similar situation exists in the cable television industry. Many cable company offices are open only from nine to five Monday through Friday, yet subscriber service needs often peak during evenings and on weekends and holidays. The lesson here is that companies often cannot—or will not—see their own shortcomings. It's easier to blame the customer—to pass off the problem as "human nature."

Paperwork that the customer has to fill out is another example of such myopia. Management and staff may find their paperwork easy to understand because, after all, the company designed the forms, and employees work with them all the time. But that's no guarantee the forms are easy for the customer to understand or fill out.

Companies need to be continuously on the lookout for such weak links in the delivery chain. It helps to start with a simple checklist of customer-interaction points and give honest answers to how you're managing those make-or-break situations. Figure 4–1 is an example of such a checklist covering three typical categories of company-customer interactions.

Any "no" or "don't know" answer on this checklist reveals a trouble spot. But even if all the answers appear to be right, this doesn't mean the company's service standard for every item on the list is satisfactory from the *customer's* viewpoint. Managers may think they have an ade-

FIGURE 4–1

Typical Checklist of Company-Customer Interactions

---

1. Telephone
   - ☐ Are there enough phone lines to handle the volume of phone calls I receive?
   - ☐ Do I have phone equipment that monitors phone calls, volume, times of day, busy signals, etc.?
   - ☐ Is there a standard for answering phone calls (within three rings?) and is it monitored?
   - ☐ Are answering personnel trained, have information they need close at hand, know the business, have authority to act?
   - ☐ Is there an 800-number, and are my phone hours reasonable for what my customers want?

2. Person-to-Person
   - ☐ Do I have enough people to handle the business when the customers are there?
   - ☐ Are employees trained? Are they told what is expected, and is it monitored?
   - ☐ Will the customer get the same consistent service even if the employee serving them is different?
   - ☐ Does the customer get the employee's full attention?
   - ☐ Is the employee polite, neat, organized, courteous, knowledgable, concerned, appreciative?
   - ☐ How are irate customers treated? Who handles them? What is that person's training and level of authority?

3. Mail
   - ☐ What is the standard response time for correspondence?
   - ☐ If a customer writes, will anything happen? Are written communications clearly understandable and customer-friendly?
   - ☐ Is all of the information provided, and is there an easy way to communicate back to the company?
   - ☐ Do we solicit complaints, and how are they handled?

---

quate standard in any given case, and everybody might be living up to the letter of the law on the checklist, but continuous monitoring is needed to see that the standards really meet customer expectations. Table 4–1 represents an excerpt from a commercial bank's "service attributes" checklist.

Note the final item in this example: *Customer complaint*. There is a big gap between what the customer wants and what the bank delivers. The customer expects that complaints should be handled within 24 hours, but the bank's standard is five working days. Granted, some complaints may involve complex problems that have to be tracked throughout the bank system, but it's not an acceptable excuse to say "these things take time," especially when the banking industry today so proudly extolls the benefits of automated, computerized systems. The customer can justifiably say, "If your star-wars technology is so terrific, why can't you push the right buttons and fix that error on my statement right now?" Bank management thinks in terms of hundreds of millions of dollars and tens or hundreds of thousands of customers; but that one customer whose checks are bouncing because a deposit didn't get credited promptly is thinking in equally great terms on a personal level. To the bank manager, a $75 bounced

TABLE 4–1

Service Attributes

Function	Timeliness	Reliability	Responsiveness
Loan request	Chief Loan Officer will meet within 5 days of lead or interest	Loan documents to credit dept. 100% accurate and complete	CLO will provide commitment/ answer within 30 days
Teller line	Limit % of time customer waits over 3 minutes	Transaction completed accurately	Teller greets, thanks, and uses customer's name
Customer complaint	Response wanted within 24 hours		All resolution of errors within 5 working days

check may seem trivial; to the customer it can mean the difference between a good or bad credit rating, buying the week's groceries, or losing insurance coverage because of a late premium payment. Even if the problem was the customer's own fault, he or she deserves a prompt explanation. Waiting five days (or longer if a weekend or holiday intervenes) can seem like an eternity to somebody who's worrying whether or not they have any money in their bank account.

The issue is *customer empathy,* and many companies are so caught up in their internal policies, procedures, and systems that managers and frontline employees forget, or never learn, how to be empathetic toward the customer. For that matter, the delivery chain itself may contain built-in barriers to empathy. This can be reflected, for example, in late-payment notices. A notice may read:

> Your account is delinquent. Please pay full amount due. Good credit depends upon prompt payment. If you have already paid, you may disregard this notice. For information about your bill, call (000) 000-0000 Monday through Friday between 9 a.m. and 5 p.m.

This notice is abrupt, cold, and accusatory. It leaves customers feeling as if they're dealing with a mindless machine—which, of course, they are because the company's automated accounts-receivable system triggered the computer to print a standard notice and routed it into the automated mass-mailing system. The argument is that such automation is needed to handle a large volume of business or to catch late-paying customers and give them a nudge before they fall too far behind. So be it; but the nudging doesn't have to be done with a sledgehammer. The notice, after all, wasn't composed by the computer. It was written by a human being, and it could have been written in a more customer-friendly style. It could more openly acknowledge the possibility that the company itself didn't properly credit the customer's account, or it could explicitly indicate that "X" days are needed for a payment to be posted once it's received. And what if the payment was lost or delayed in the mail? If the customer actually mailed the payment a week ago, it isn't very reassuring to be told simply: "If you have already paid, you may disregard this notice." Consider, also, the prospect that you're dealing here with a long-time, loyal customer with a good payment record and that this is the first time—or one of the very few times—when their payment has been late. Maybe they were on vacation at bill-paying time last month, or maybe they've had a serious personal problem, such a a death in the family, that took them from their normal routine. If somebody has diligently paid their bills with you on time for the last six or eight years, and the first time they're late they get an insensitive computer-generated warning, their loyalty to your company may be suddenly and seriously diminished. The message you've sent them suggests, "We don't really appreciate your loyalty; in fact, we don't even *know* about it."

There are at least three other trouble spots in the typical late-payment notice cited above. For one thing, there is no good reason to remind people today that "good credit depends upon prompt payment." This is a condescending remark to any adult who is already in a position to be buying on credit. Secondly, if the customer has already paid this bill, there is a conspicuous lack of a "thank-you." The only message is that "you may disregard this notice." Finally, the customer is told that if they want to discuss the bill, they should call a certain number within specified hours, and they are given a long-distance area code. For many people, nine-to-five on Monday through Friday is the least convenient period to make such calls, and the company might well consider scheduling account information phone service at more customer-friendly hours. As for the telephone area code, if the company is doing business long distance, it should install toll-free "800" numbers for customer information and complaint handling.

A good and long-standing customer expects a reciprocal relationship with the company. The customer demonstrates good will through repeat buying and on-time payments, and the company is expected to reciprocate with some good will of its own. It might be an overstatement to call this arrangement a "friendship," but most of us *do* feel more kindly toward a company that treats us like a friend. We like to think that our business is appreciated and that we represent something more than a speck on a computer chip or a name on a mailing list. That's why it's important that a company's delivery chain or customer-interaction process—no matter how much it is automated and computerized—be designed to allow for the personal touch, to accommodate exceptions, and to show real responsiveness to the unique needs of individual customers. This is everybody's responsibility, but the many separate activities affecting the make-or-break points in a customer relationship have to be pulled together, synchronized, and managed as a whole. In the absence of a chief service officer (CSO), this overseer task in most companies falls under the aegis of what we call "operations management."

Operations managers, or whoever their counterparts are from one company to the next, should ensure good communications among all the departments within the company and between the company and its key outside suppliers. Sometimes this job can be accomplished informally, but many times it requires more formal, structured agreements and firmly established guidelines. For example, if data processing is late with billing, there may be a spin-off problem with phone answering in the customer-service department, where the phone lines will be clogged by customers inquiring about their bills. Such a problem can be mitigated or avoided altogether if there is good communication between data processing and the phone-answering department, and especially if a fail-safe or "exception" agreement has been worked out in advance between the two departments. In a small company, the solution could be as simple as having the data-processing manager call the phone-service manager to say, "We're going to be a couple of days late getting the bills out, so you'll probably want to put on some extra phone people next week." This assumes, of course, that the data-processing manager can tell in advance when there's going to be a problem. But if that isn't the case, there should still be some provision for a quick response when the problem comes up.

Operations managers always have to be alert to the customer-satisfaction implications of *all* of the company's standard procedures and policies. In a certain airline reservations office, phone answerers had an hourly quota of calls based on a two-minute maximum talk-time per call. In trying to meet the quota, however, employees tended to rush the customers through each call and often cut people short because the standard two minutes was up. The company was trying legitimately to monitor and manage the productivity of its phone answerers, but in this case, the quota was counterproductive because it seriously undercut the quality of service delivery. Customers were angered at being hurried through a call that was important to them, and the harried employees often sounded curt and impatient.

One of the most persistent problems in retailing and service industries is having enough people available to handle peak periods of customer demand. Most companies know what their normal cycles are, and they staff accordingly. But there are understaffing situations that some companies continue to manage badly, and there are times when even the best-run companies come up short because they didn't plan for the exception. The data-processing/phone-answering example cited earlier is one of those situations. Another example is a cellular phone company whose customer billings had become so complicated that it was swamped with inquiries and complaints for several days at the end of each monthly billing period. Accounting and phone-answering personnel were overwhelmed with work at these times, and customers were exasperated in their efforts to get answers. The solution was actually simple. The company went from a once-a-month billing cycle to five times a month. An individual customer was still billed only once every month, but the company's billing process was spread out over five periods, smoothing the workload and easing the pressure on billing department employees. The company also got its billing vendor to help redesign the invoices and statements to make them easier for the customer to understand, and this helped reduce the number of phone inquiries at each billing period.

Marketing

We've established that getting new customers is only part of marketing's job. Equally important are the ways in which marketing can support the rest of the company in serving and keeping customers.

For starters, the marketing budget should be split into two categories: (1) dollars spent on acquiring customers, and (2) dollars spent on keeping customers. There will be some overlapping because the same dollar in any given case may serve both purposes. But it's important for marketers and senior management to quantify the two basic roles separately, both for practical budgeting purposes and to ensure that the customer-retention role is given due recognition. Once everybody has achieved this double-mission mindset, and the money has been allocated accordingly, marketing can support the service-delivery and retention programs in many creative and practical ways. The following are several key areas of concern for which marketing should take ongoing responsibility:

1. Ensure easy access by customers into the company. For example, see that telephone directory listings are written or indexed the way the customer would think about them instead of the way the company is organized, and purify all customer-targeted messages of company jargon.

2. Make sure that new product or service introductions are well-understood internally before the customer ever sees them. Many customer-contact employees

complain that the customer knows more than they do about a new product or service. Since marketing creates customer appeal for new products, it should also communicate that appeal to employees and ensure that they are well-enough informed to discuss the product with customers.

3. Develop high-frequency customer input. Assume that top management will *not* regularly get out to listen to the customer and that marketing must provide the conduit. Allocate marketing dollars to ongoing customer-service surveys, and design attractive, easy-to-use customer-comment devices. Perform lost-customer analyses, and provide feedback to managers and employees in an easily readable format.

4. Study all customer complaints for information on product, service, and people problems. In many companies, marketing is outside the complaint loop. Maybe the reason is that marketing's role is to paint the best picture of a company, and since complaints are generally perceived as "bad news," marketing people don't want to know about them. However, complaints should be vital intelligence to marketing. They can tell you more than dozens of focus groups will because they represent reality rather than mere potential.

5. Know the exact behavior patterns and hot buttons of the top 20-percent—customers who, when they leave, take with them a disproportionate share of business. All customers, of course, should get good service, but high-value customers should be treated as if they were about to be courted away. To the frontline employee, who is often forced to follow standard procedures and policies, the high-value customer gets the lowest common denominator of service.

In many companies, more up-front marketing efforts should be aimed explicitly at getting new customer relationships off on the right foot. There are moments and events immediately following a sale, or following it for some time down the road, where the sale can collapse for lack of adequate back-up. It should be at least partly a marketing responsibility to see that this doesn't happen. For example, when a new bank checking account is opened, the customer is told to expect his or her personalized checks within a certain time. But if those checks don't arrive as promised, or if they arrive with errors in the customer's name, address, or phone number, the life-expectancy of the sale could be diminished. Right from the start, the customer has been inconvenienced, and the bank's credibility has been compromised. Since most people would rather avoid the hassle of opening another account at a different bank—especially so soon after they've been through that ordeal—there's a good chance the account will stay in place for at least a while. However, the seeds of doubt have been sown, so the next service breakdown, such as an inaccurate statement or bounced checks due to the bank's error, might be the last straw for that customer. Meanwhile, there's potential damage from having the customer telling friends and associates about the poor service. Some call this the "cocktail party index," but in more prosaic language it's known as "word-of-mouth." Research shows that, depending upon the line of trade, customers tell anywhere from eight to fifteen other people about a bad purchase or service experience, but that they will tell only two or three about a *good* experience. Studies done by General Electric reveal that word-of-mouth information circulated by satisfied consumers is at least twice as effective as paid advertising. Other research indicates that when a company receives a letter of complaint, it might as well assume that letter represents as many as 27 dissatisfied customers. One customer got miffed enough to actually sit down and write, while 26 others didn't take the trouble; they just took their business elsewhere.

Marketing, sales, and promotion personnel are supposed to have the skills and should have the motivation to help with, or at least monitor, many of the follow-up details that can put the seal on the sale. Regardless of who is given the job, there are any number of simple but effective actions that will show customers the company really cares about what happens to them. In the bank example, somebody can call the customer a day after the new checks are supposed to arrive and ask whether the checks arrived and if they were printed correctly. After the first statement is sent, somebody can call and ask whether it's accurate and if the customer needs anything explained. On the first anniversary of the account's opening, another phone call (or letter) might ask: "Are you pleased with our service? What can we do better? Can we advise you on anything involving finances or perhaps help you with some major purchase you're planning to make?"

It's really neither complicated nor especially costly for companies to concentrate on the little things that mean a lot: things like letters of appreciation for long-term business, thank-you notes for major purchases, friendly acknowledgment for the final payment on a loan or installment contract, and phone calls or letters asking if the customer is satisfied and soliciting advice on how to improve service. In most cases, the apparatus and resources to do such things are already there. Increasingly, computerized customer files typically contain not only names, addresses, and phone numbers, but also such buyer-behavior and demographic information as a history of purchases or account activity, age, income, number of people in the household, make and year of automobile, and so on. If this information doesn't exist in one consolidated file, there are ways to cross-index from the firm's total database to build customer profiles either individually or by segments based on common characteristics. From there, it is possible to create tickler files and calendars of retention-marketing activities.

Beyond such immediate retention-marketing value, customer databases are useful research tools for monitoring broad changes in customer behavior and for furnishing early-warning signs of potential churn problems. When correlated with financial data, including marketing and service costs, they can also enable a firm to calculate the incremental value of keeping a customer for an additional month, year, or number and dollar volume of purchases— or, conversely, an opportunity to assess the cost of losing a customer.

Given a real understanding and total commitment from top management, the operational leadership (and consequently many of the technical capabilities for customer retention) should be drawn from the marketing, sales, promotion, and market research arms of the business. Additional help can be obtained from outside advertising and public relations agencies, market research companies, service consultants, direct-mail specialists, and even printing and graphics firms. And although some of the tools, methods, and events may seem rather humdrum or mechanical when viewed from the executive suite or a middle manager's office, we must remember that the customer's constantly shifting, evolving perception of the company is formulated mainly from an accumulation of *little* things and episodic interactions. Good customer service depends upon systematic, continuous attention to these mechanics and details. For example:

1. Are application forms, questionnaires, form letters, and customer notices sensibly organized, intelligibly written, attractively designed and customer friendly?

2. Do overdue payment notices reflect a posture of shooting first and asking questions later? Or do they give the customer the benefit of a doubt, leaving open the possibility of a mere oversight or a mix-up in billing? Do they make customers feel as if they might be dealing with people who break legs over late payments, or do they demonstrate a fair-minded, friendly concern and possibly a willingness to negotiate easier terms?

3. Do the company's written or printed communications project a consistent image, or are they all over the waterfront in graphic style, tone of language, and quality of preparation?

4. Does the company have—or has it considered—a toll-free customer helpline that is separate from the "800" sales number? If such a line exists, is it adequately staffed with competent personnel, and does it operate at times that are convenient to customers?

5. Are the company's complaint-handling policies and procedures geared mainly toward absorbing noise and reducing nuisance levels, or are they structured to deliver customer satisfaction, create customer retention opportunities, and collect information about service levels?

6. Are sales, marketing, advertising, promotion, and market research personnel tuned in to the customer complaint system? Do they have the opportunity and motivation to use complaint records to identify product and service problems and to help develop better policies and procedures?

7. Does the company use, or has it considered using, orientation or information kits for new customers (or for dealer, suppliers, and other third parties)?

8. When acquisition marketing pulls new customers in the door, or when special sale events and promotions generate heavier-than-usual traffic, does the company ensure adequate staffing to take care of the extra business?

9. Under normal circumstances, is staff scheduling in line with the regular, predictable peaks and valleys in customer traffic? Do personnel stand idle during part of the day, and customers stand in line during rush hours?

10. Do the company's hours of operation match its customers' hours of greatest need? Do customers have

to take time out of their own workdays to do business with you, and do they find your doors closed and your phones unanswered when they need you the most?

The marketing department cannot bear primary responsibility for all of these areas, but marketing's understanding of customer behavior qualifies it to contribute ideas and act as an advocate, expediter, and watchdog to see that customer interests are addressed at every step.

Human Resources

Human resource, or personnel, departments contain many important links in the delivery chain because they influence the makeup and morale of a company's workforce.

At the outset, the personnel department has to find and hire the right people for customer contact and service jobs. Some people are good at dealing with the public, while other do better working behind the scenes; it's personnel's responsibility to detect these differences and place employees in the right jobs. Customer contact work requires people who thrive on doing many things at once and who can endure the stress of handling a continuous parade of customers with different personalities and demands. Backroom work, on the other hand, requires people who are conscientious about details and who take pride in doing the same job right time after time. Many companies have developed pre-employment profiles to screen job applicants for these varying traits before hiring them. In today's workplace, where job satisfaction is an important motivator, and in today's marketplace, where employee performance is a key to customer satisfaction, it's critical that companies arrange the right "marriage" between the job and the person. Neither the company nor the customer benefits if a low-adaptor person is put in a fast-paced, multifunctional job. The employee will burn out, and the customers will turn off.

An intelligent person would not buy a car and then fail to check the oil, replace worn parts, or take it in for warranty inspections. Yet companies hire new employees, give them minimal training, and then fail to go back and check on what needs to be fixed. This is a problem that in most companies should fall under the job description of the personnel, or human resources, department—or at least should be coordinated by such a department. In some companies, personnel departments occasionally conduct employee attitude surveys to get feedback on such issues as benefits or management communication. Rarely, however, does anyone ask employees whether they have the right tools or resources to serve their customers well.

Employee rewards and recognition are also essential for good service delivery, and the personnel department should ensure that management recognizes and rewards employees who help keep customers.

Historically, personnel management has been a rather quiet, even passive function. Unless personnel administrators got involved in relations with organized labor, their jobs were low-profile compared to those of most other managers. Personnel departments were largely maintenance centers for keeping employee records, updating policy manuals on orders from above, maintaining vacation schedules, and processing paperwork for benefit claims. But all that is rapidly changing under the mandate of government regulations and the pressures of special interests. The focus now is on employee rights, affirmative action, special considerations for child-bearing women, and a wide variety of other employee support programs. Personnel specialists have to play a far more proactive role today than in years past, and this gives them greater visibility and influence with the workforce. From this new and enhanced vantage point, personnel departments bear increased responsibility for employee attitudes and behavior that directly affect quality and customer service. Charles Aubrey of Banc One says, "Employee behavioral standards are the biggest challenge to quality improvement . . . even more challenging than getting the physical environment right."

Whether it's called "personnel administration" or "human resources," the role of cultivating and supporting positive attitudes and personal satisfaction among employees is a vital part of the quality mix.

Every Manager's Job

The best managers try to meddle as little as possible in the jobs their subordinates are doing. They strive to do their own jobs right the first time, while instilling that same ethic in their subordinates and peers. In customer-retention management, this philosophy of "letting go" is especially important. It means letting go enough so that the people closest to the customers can do their jobs right. Empowering clerks to make refunds or authorizing cash-wrap personnel to make exceptions for the customer's benefit are examples of putting decisions in the hands of people who are best positioned to make them. Wise management also knows that when you diffuse responsibility in this way, you must also see that sufficient resources are in place to make the system work. That includes both financial and human resources, and it includes motivating and rewarding people to accept responsibility. Furthermore, while customer service is rightfully everybody's job, people must be made aware of the specific contributions expected of them as individuals.

At McDonald's, for example, the watchword for customer service is *consistency*. The company wants its customers to always know what to expect and to always rely on having that expectation met at the same level every time they go to the counter or drive-by order window. Getting this kind of consistency, however, requires rigorous employee training and explicit procedures. While employees are trained, motivated, and rewarded for friendliness and courtesy, they are also required to follow step-by-step procedures and do their job the *same way* with every customer. For example, McDonald's training steps and operating procedures for breakfast service look like the following:

Step 1: Greet Customer.
1. Wish customer a pleasant "good morning" and do so with a cheerful smile.
2. When asking for order, do so courteously. Please give a friendly greeting to let your customers know you are there to help them.
3. Call regular customers by name. It says to them, "You are important." Recognition adds the dimension of warmth to an otherwise cold business transaction.

Step 2: Take Order.
1. Register order into the cash register as customer is giving it.
2. Be thoroughly familiar with all items on the menu.
3. Answer each question the customer may ask about ingredients, food freshness, content, and handling time.
4. If you receive orders for items we do not carry, suggest a similar or related menu item. Do not say, "We don't carry that particular product."
5. Be particularly helpful with detailed explanations to new customers, and they will become repeat customers.
6. If a customer orders an item after the breakfast period has ended, explain politely that this practice is necessary to provide quality service and fresh food.
7. Suggest only one addition item to your customer. That person will appreciate it. For example, "How about a nice hot Danish to go with that steaming hot cup of coffee?"
8. Accept special orders graciously.

This type of by-the-numbers service strategy has reaped legendary success for McDonald's, and it can work well for many other businesses that offer a fairly limited range of products or services to a large volume or steady stream of customers. For different businesses, however, the emphasis often has to be placed on customized service that allows employees more freedom in deciding how to deal with each customer. The Nordstrom Department Store organization is one such example. Nordstrom salespeople are recruited, trained, and rewarded according to their ability to work more autonomously. The employee performance rule at Nordstrom states, "Use common sense and satisfy the customer."

It is not enough for companies to think or even talk about keeping customers. Every action, every daily task, and every communication must project the retention message. And all departments or groups within a company, regardless of their specialties, can contribute to or detract from the mission. The key to having everyone contribute is *coordination*.

Bringing all the parts together into a coordinated customer-retention program requires careful planning that should start with a complete service audit. Everything that can affect customer satisfaction has to be mapped out and examined for strengths and weaknesses. Figure 4–2 represents a schematic model for doing such an audit and laying the groundwork for a good customer retention strategy.

Each of the eight subjects surrounding the center circle in this model represents an important area of investigation, planning, and ongoing stewardship. Senior management should question the company's mission, strategy, policies, operating procedures, and results in each area.

Cultural Change

- Is the company's culture conducive to customer satisfaction and retention?
- What are senior management's highest priorities: maximizing short-term profits? rapid growth or

FIGURE 4–2

Customer Retention Strategy Model

expansion? impressing stock analysts? holding the line against competition? creating value and satisfaction for customers?

- Does the company have a high, low, or so-so quality image in the marketplace?
- Are employees motivated and loyal, or is there high employee turnover?
- Is employee training viewed as a productive investment or simply a necessary expense?

- Do employees get bonuses for high-quality performance, and are there other (non-monetary) rewards for customer retention?
- Does the company budget explicitly for quality improvement and customer retention?

Service Quality and Satisfaction

- Are customer satisfaction and quality-improvement objectives clearly defined?
- Does the firm regularly survey customers about product or service quality?
- Are customer requirements communicated throughout the delivery chain?
- Are suppliers brought into the quality process?
- Has the cost of poor quality and service breakdowns been quantified?
- Are there explicit performance standards for such customer-contact points as complaint handling, telephone answering, written communications, waiting time in lines, and so on?
- Are performance standards continuously monitored, and are employees regularly evaluated on their performance?
- Does the company strive for product perfection and 100 percent error-free service?

Database Research

- Does the company maintain a customer database?
- Is the database organized by market segments, niches, and high-value customers?
- Does the company know the "lifetime" value of its customers?
- What are the signs that a customer may be leaving, and is the database capable of sounding an alarm?
- Does the database track customer churn, and does it highlight the reasons why customers leave?

Customer Feedback

- Are employees trained to recognize and interpret "natural" feedback from customers?
- Does the company systematically solicit customer feedback?
- Is it easy and inviting for customers to offer feedback?
- Does the company try to follow up with customers who have left?

Complaint Handling

- Are there standard guidelines for handling customer complaints?
- Are customer-contact employees trained in complaint handling?
- Can most employees resolve routine or minor complaints on the spot?
- Does the company follow the "sunset" rule for resolving complaints quickly?
- If there is a formal or fixed complaint department, is it customer-friendly?
- Does the company track and analyze all complaints so as to pinpoint trends or trouble-spots?

High-Value

- Does the company identify its high-value customers on a systematic basis?
- Are employees alerted as to who the high-value customers are?
- Do high-value customers receive special services or privileges (such as advance notice of promotions and special sales, or easy access to top management)?
- Does the company survey its high-value customers separately from mass surveys or in regard to special questions or problems?

Outreach/Competition

- Does the company continuously and systematically study its competition?
- How does the company compare to its competition in terms of product and service quality, personnel, budget, marketplace image, etc.?
- What are the relative strengths and weaknesses of the competition?
- What are consumers' perceptions of the competition (does the company survey competitors' customers as well as its own)?

"Glue" of Multiple Products

For a company that markets more than one product or service:

- Is the database segmented by product?
- Are advertising and promotion segmented by product?
- Does the company have an "umbrella" image for quality in all of its products and services, or is it considered good at some things and bad at others?
- How much cross selling is done, and is it possible to do more?
- Are employees better motivated regarding certain products or services than they are for others—and if so, is this in line with the company's marketing strategy and goals?
- If the company does poorly with certain products or services, might it be advisable to drop them and concentrate on what the firm can do best?

It may seem repetitive, but we can't say it too often: superior quality and outstanding customer service cannot be created or maintained without a concentrated, coordinated effort from *all* segments of the organization.

Delivering true customer satisfaction requires true teamwork. Leon Gorman, president of L. L. Bean, didn't flinch from being repetitious when he told *Fortune* magazine that customer service is "just a day-in, day-out, ongoing, never-ending, unremitting, persevering, compassionate type of activity." L. L. Bean is known for just the kind of pervasive commitment to customer satisfaction that Gorman describes, and that commitment has paid off handsomely. The company even goes so far as to maintain a roster of customers whose feet don't match in size so that L. L. Bean can assemble mixed-size pairs of shoes for them.

Building and sustaining such a customer-conscious operation is hard to do, but there are intelligent ways to go about it, starting with a thorough service audit. From the findings of the audit, management can formulate a strategy and construct plans for carrying out that strategy. After that, it all depends upon following through with every little detail. Rubbermaid's chairman, Stanley Gault, says it's a matter of "basic consideration, time, effort, commitment, and follow-up."

In the early going, some people won't easily join the spirit of the program. Employees may be skeptical about management's intentions or may balk at being shaken out of their routines. Suppliers may resent what they think is unwarranted meddling in the way they do business. And management itself is often divided. Charles Aubrey of Banc One says that line managers aren't always supportive of quality-improvement efforts. Some of them are uncomfortable at seeing the traditional vertical management system tipped to the horizontal, participative style that a total-quality program requires. However, if top management persistently reinforces the quality message and delivers the necessary incentives, tools, and support systems, people's attitudes will change, and the quality fever will spread.

5

THE ONGOING COMMITMENT

THE BEST companies—those most distinguished for their ability to keep customers—are *never satisfied*.

Donald Petersen said it wasn't important where Ford was when it began its turnaround program; what was important was the need to focus on *continuous* improvement. Ford learned this principle by studying Japanese manufacturers to see what had given them such an edge over Americans. The Japanese advantage did not lie in technology or a superior work ethic, but was based on a dedication to continuous improvement. Japanese manufacturers believe there is no such thing as an acceptable level of quality below 100 percent and that you're in trouble if you start letting yourself think you've reached perfection.

The concept of continuous improvement may appear simple on the surface, but it requires a way of thinking and an intensity of commitment that are unfamiliar to many American businesspeople. We tend to set goals, track our progress toward those goals, and then feel satisfied when we've reached them. But being satisfied means that we've stopped moving ahead. A sales quota has been met; a productivity level has been attained; a return on investment ratio has been reached; and now everything is working just fine. We are good at this sort of scorekeeping, but in business the game is never over.

There is no question that goal setting and scorekeeping are needed to stimulate and measure continuous improvement in quality, and we can apply many of the same standards and measurement techniques used for other business purposes. Many companies are satisfied with measuring one or two facets of their customer service every now and then. But these sporadic efforts can be worse than useless. They are often misleading because they fail to reveal steady, long-term trends. Frequently, they are viewed as ends in themselves, and management takes no follow-up action. They can also send the wrong signals to middle management and frontline employees if they are used primarily to light occasional fires. And worse, they can undercut morale if used as hammers over the heads of middle managers or as a means of highlighting unfavorable comparisons in the short-term performance of different groups within the company. The key is that continuous improvement requires continuous and consistent measurement followed up by real action.

There are many types of useful measurements that can be done internally or by outside agents such as service consultants or research firms that specialize in customer attitudes and behavior. Surveys can measure customer response at any interaction point in the delivery chain. Research can show why customers leave under any given circumstance; it can measure gaps between customer expectations and company reality; and it can reveal the differences between what customers want and what employees think they want. Depending upon the company or type of industry, other specific areas that lend themselves to continuous measurement include:

1. Telephone-answering quality
2. Waiting time in lines
3. Convenience of business hours
4. Promptness in responding to complaints
5. Product or service knowledge of frontline employees
6. Time required to process new-customer paperwork
7. Simplicity of forms that customers must fill out
8. Readability of printed customer instructions
9. Clarity of interior signage
10. Bottlenecks in customer traffic flow
11. Convenience and ease of access to special customer services or facilities such as restrooms, telephones, gift-wrap departments, and fitting rooms

Table 5–1 presents a sample survey used by a West Coast department store to measure its customer satisfaction levels in selected areas of service delivery against those of seven competitors. The figures represent only the percentage of customers who gave the two highest ratings ("excellent" or "good") on each service attribute at each store. While this survey was not conducted or sponsored by Nordstrom, Inc., it clearly shows the favorable results of Nordstrom's customer-satisfaction strategy that we've discussed elsewhere.

Continuous scrutiny of all such links in the delivery chain is absolutely essential. But the scrutiny alone is a futile exercise unless management really understands the findings. Many companies collect data and disseminate it throughout the management hierarchy; but then there it sits, waiting to be filed in front of the last such report. A study may show, for example, that 45 percent of a company's customers have been very satisfied with service for the past 18 months. If this equals or betters the performance of competitors during the same period, management may conclude that everything is okay or maybe even

TABLE 5–1

Department Store Customer Satisfaction Rating
(by shoppers of each store)

Question: How would you rate each of these stores on the following characteristics?

% Giving Highest Two Ratings	*Survey Sponsor & Other Competitors*							*NORDSTROM*
Selling Service Performance								
Salespeople thank me or show appreciation when I make a purchase	59%	61%	58%	42%	56%	56%	60%	78%
Salespeople are knowledgeable about the merchandise.	53	59	58	36	55	52	57	80
Salespeople seem glad to help me with a return or exchange.	46	52	45	30	50	45	45	71
The store has enough salespeople.	43	52	49	26	40	43	45	75
Salespeople seem to enjoy their work.	42	52	48	30	38	42	50	77
I usually don't have to wait in line—the actual ringing of a sale is quick and easy.	41	55	48	25	30	40	50	72
Salespeople seem genuinely interested in helping me. They go out of their way for me.	40	54	48	26	39	40	46	76
Salespeople acknowledge me when I enter their department.	39	54	49	29	40	41	47	77

TABLE 5–1

continued

Salespeople make suggestions about other merchandise they think I might be interested in.	35	51	43	23	31	35	40	73
Selling service average:	44%	54%	49%	30%	42%	43%	48%	75%

Store Appearance & Merchandise

Merchandise in this store is housed in attractive, up-to-date surroundings.	72%	73%	72%	52%	68%	63%	65%	83%
The floors and carpeting are kept neat and clean.	72	74	70	56	72	65	64	82
The store usually carries merchandise of the quality and taste that I am looking for.	68	72	69	2	65	60	63	80
Merchandise is organized and labeled so I can find what I am looking for.	61	66	65	45	66	59	60	77
I get good fashion ideas from displays in this store. They tempt me to buy.	60	68	65	45	59	56	52	79
Store appearance & merchandise average:	67%	70%	68%	50%	66%	61%	61%	80%

(continued on page 136

outstanding. But this would be merely running in place. The question arises, "Was that 45-percent satisfaction rate better than the company's own rate the last time a survey was done?" If it wasn't, then there's no reason to be pleased. It isn't enough to be just as good as or somewhat better than your competition, especially if the comparison is based on a single survey. By the time the study

TABLE 5–1

continued

	Prices and Advertising								
The store usually has what it advertises.	65%	64%	62%	52%	72%	62%	55%		74%
Advertised sales values are honest.	63	62	60	52	74	64	55		71
Prices are competitive with identical or similar merchandise in other stores.	57	54	54	52	71	59	51		63
Prices & advertising average	62%	60%	58%	52%	72%	62%	54%		69%

is completed and passed around for review, one of your competitors may have overtaken you. The only reason to celebrate is if your customer satisfaction level is steadily improving, and the only way you can tell that is by continuously charting your performance.

Customer satisfaction measurements are road signs to help keep us going in the right direction. They also serve as mileage markers to show how far we've progressed toward a current goal. But the journey in this case is endless; there will always be more miles to travel.

Continuing the Job

How can you ensure that you stay on course once you've started on the path to improved service? Chapter 4 dealt with how each part of the organization and each function needs to be refocused on keeping customers. Old job responsibilities, titles, and organizational structures are not always in tune with this objective.

To get the proper focus, a new high-level executive position should be created: the *Chief Service Officer* (CSO). Most presidents and CEOs rise through the ranks of traditional divisions such as finance, marketing, or engineering, but these typical career paths hardly ever pass through customer-service territory. The dominant thinking and policy making thus remain rooted in traditional concerns, and nobody bears top-level responsibility or wields significant power to bring together all the resources needed for customer retention. With few exceptions, senior management titles in *Fortune* 1000 companies don't include the words "customer service" or "quality." If jobs representing those responsibilities exist, they are almost always beneath the top-management echelon. The people who *are* at the top customarily argue that this doesn't mean anything, because "customer satisfaction is everybody's business." But this doesn't reflect reality in most companies. When customer service responsibility is shared as a part-time or ancillary duty by people as busy as most CEOs, presidents, and executive vice presidents, the job simply isn't getting done in a systematic fashion. Neither is there any true, traceable accountability. Since customer retention is now a survival issue, it only makes sense that the job be given to a specialist with the senior management rank and clout that it takes to get things accomplished. That specialist would be the CSO, and his or her very existence would be a signal to employees and customers that the company is "dead serious" about service. The CSO can be the *one* person who ensures that all operations and service-contact points are focused on customer expectations and needs. This new officer would work with all divisions to apply the necessary resources to service problems and customer retention opportunities. He or she would be, in effect, a "resident customer"— not merely an ombudsman or advocate who cuts through red tape and solves problems piecemeal—but a high-level manager who keeps a vigilant eye on service levels and policies that affect service delivery.

Part of the job would be to help evaluate new products and services before they're introduced, and another important part would be screening all customer forms and paperwork for clarity, tone, ease of handling, and appropriateness to the company's desired service image.

The CSO would play an important role with employees, too. Since employee morale depends partly upon having the right tools to deliver good service, the CSO would be the voice for employees who are frustrated at not having those tools. Likewise, the CSO would monitor all divisions and departments to see that appropriate recognition systems are in place and that high-performance employees are not being slighted.

Other basic responsibilities and powers assigned to the CSO would include the following:

1. Advocating, as a primary corporate goal, the need to *keep* customers as well as acquire new ones.

2. Articulating the vision and mission of quality service in terms that are clearly understandable to senior management, middle management, and employees.

3. Identifying what business the customer thinks the company is in, and determining what level of service customers expect in that business.

4. Evaluating the impact every policy and procedure in the company has on customers.

5. Developing a comprehensive strategic plan, including timetables, for improving service levels.

6. Helping all divisions and departments of the company set explicit service-level goals and develop workable tracking and measuring techniques.

7. Developing systems and methods for collecting customer feedback, and ensuring that such feedback is constantly transmitted in clear terms to all levels of management.

8. Evaluating all training, orientation, and management-development programs to see that they emphasize service quality and customer satisfaction.

9. Encouraging frontline employees to contribute feedback on service delivery and customer satisfac-

tion, and ensuring that employees have easy, risk-free means of reporting such feedback.

10. Bearing ultimate responsibility for resolving customer complaints.

11. Analyzing customer complaints to detect and remove any persistent barriers to good service.

12. Knowing the service levels of all competitors.

13. Studying other industries to learn new approaches and better ideas for service delivery.

14. Evaluating the service and product quality of suppliers, and assessing the impact of suppliers' service levels on the company's own delivery of service.

On the basis of these general responsibilities and levels of authority, we can develop a more formal CSO job description such as the one shown in Figure 5–1.

Having developed a job description for the CSO, we now face the question of qualifications. What kind of person is needed for the job? What should their education, work experience, and aptitudes be?

Picking the right person can be difficult because there are few role models to choose from within traditional company structures. Many companies have people they might call "customer service managers" or something similar. Ordinarily, these people are supervisors or lower-level managers in charge of complaint handling, phone answering, or some other activity that the company associates with customer service. But they are generally low-paid and not trained for much responsibility beyond what they're already carrying. If there is a temptation to pick one of these people for CSO because "they've had customer-service experience," it should be avoided. That level of experience is worlds apart from the CSO's job.

In setting the qualifications for the CSO, we should ask the same questions that would be asked when selecting any other senior executive. Ideally, a CSO should represent an amalgam of experience and training. In order to

FIGURE 5–1

Sample Job Description for Chief Service Officer

Title: Chief Service Officer

Reports to: Chief Executive Officer, Chairman

Organization: _____

- Create customer service department.
- Hire and develop department staff.
- Develop and monitor annual customer service department budget.
- Manage centralized customer-help telephone directory.
- Manage customer relations.
- Set objectives for customer service performance.
- Establish company-wide service goals for all levels of customer contact.
- Develop and implement service award system to recognize excellence in employee performance.
- Act as customer service information and support service.

Training:

- Assist human resource department in writing training objectives based on customer feedback (complaints, interviews, comment cards).
- Help to develop content of customer service manager's training.
- Work with business units to develop customer service programs.
- Evaluate effectiveness of training programs based on customer service needs.

Customer contact:

- Identify all customer contact areas.
- Develop customer-driven service objectives.
- Help set performance standards based on *always* meeting customers' needs.
- Determine and implement standards for telephone service.
- Ensure that the vision of quality service is communicated to the employees.
- Coordinate and implement customer service procedures and policies.
- Work closely with customer service managers to determine service deficiencies, and evaluate needs for improvement.
- Work with operating units in developing action plans to improve service performance.

FIGURE 5–1

continued

- Help customer-service task force groups to identify problem areas.
- Create Corrective Action Teams (CATs) to fix problem areas.
- Develop and monitor complaint handling procedures.
- Resolve customer complaints and inquiries in a timely manner.

Technological Development:

- Design management tools to regularly measure existing levels of service company-wide.
- Develop and implement measurement techniques to identify trends and potential problem areas.
- Anticipate and respond to customer-service needs on new products and services.
- Help develop evaluations for employee product knowledge and service.

Management Presence/Strategic Planning:

- Develop a customer service mission statement.
- Create a customer-friendly climate by setting customer-driven service goals.
- Conduct needs assessments with focus group customer forums.
- Monitor competition and industry developments.
- Evaluate other industries for service ideas.
- Help establish suggestion/idea referral program.
- Ensure continual visibility and importance of quality service to the board of directors and all management.
- Communicate with industry stock analysts and other corporate constituencies about service levels.
- Evaluate the profitability of service delivery and the expense of nonconformance to customers' requirements.

---

work with and improve internal procedures and processes, he or she should have a keen understanding of the operations side of the business. A financial background, or at least more than a passing acquaintance with finance, will help in calculating and tracking the cost of losing customers and the profitability of keeping them; and it's important, too, that the CSO be able to communicate well with financial specialists and have credibility with other top executives when it comes to money matters.

Another key requirement is an understanding of the use of research. The CSO needn't be an expert on research methods but certainly has to know what to ask for and how to interpret and communicate the results.

If there is a single background that might be considered most fertile for the development of a CSO, it would probably be marketing. Marketers are good communicators and observers, and they know how to find their way around a company. They also understand the customer, keep tabs on the competition, work with research, sell their ideas to top management, and develop marketing budgets. Most people reaching executive status through the marketing ranks will have the necessary customer orientation and will have been exposed to many of the same day-to-day demands that the CSO will face.

While a marketing background covers many of the qualifications for CSO, it is also important that the candidate have line experience. Other managers tend to have little respect for senior officers who haven't paid their dues— who haven't done at least a little time in the trenches— and if the position of CSO is to have any real meaning, it has to command respect at all levels of management. The CSO also has to know personally what it's really like out in the ranks where people work day after day with the fussy details and fight the brush fires that are always breaking out.

The position of CSO is truly a *senior* position, but it cannot be treated as a career cul-de-sac for topped-out executives from other divisions. Appointment to the job should be seen as an honor, and the position must carry major policy-making power. In fact, the CSO should be someone who might be considered for chief executive officer or chairman at some later point.

Titles notwithstanding, many companies are actually run by a "management committee" made up of the top few senior officers, and the CSO should be a member of that committee, sitting alongside the CEO, president, and executive vice presidents from key divisions. An argument can even be made for giving the CSO a certain degree of veto power over other committee members. Controllers or chief financial officers in many companies already have such power, reporting straight to the board of directors as virtually independent guardians of the company's financial health. Considering that there wouldn't be any financial health to worry about if it weren't for customers, the CSO might also report directly to the board on the company's *service* health.

One more broad qualification for the CSO's job is the ability to influence the company's culture on a major scale. The ideal CSO today would be someone who's already been that route: someone who has played a key role in revolutionizing a corporate culture and is experienced at persuading other key decisionmakers to support the effort. Chairpersons, CEOs, presidents, and other senior executives have to believe in the need for change and must contribute their own talents and prestige if a cultural revolution is to succeed or even get off the ground. The right CSO can and should act as a catalyst, strategist, coach, coordinator, and monitor in helping to bring about such a revolution.

A few years into the future, after the concept of the CSO has been more widely accepted, a pattern of career-path development for the job will emerge. Companies will begin to create developmental channels and start grooming candidates for the role; furthermore, business college curricula will include courses or whole study programs to teach the necessary skills and perspectives for the job. Until then, good CSOs will probably be hard to find, and companies that are dedicated to winning will compete intensely in the pool of available talent.

Generally Accepted Service Principles (GASP)^{TM}

American businesses face a growing burden of social accountability. Companies, whether publicly or privately held, are expected to be much better "citizens" than they used to be. They are asked or ordered to clean up and protect the environment. They are increasingly pressured to support cultural and social activities. And many of the larger companies are expected to offer day-care services for employees with children, to pay for drug and alcohol rehabilitation programs, to operate employee fitness centers, to provide inner-city school tutoring, and to support an ever growing assortment of other special interests. In short, managers can no longer manage purely for the sake of profits and growth. Success in business today is not measured solely by the famous bottom line on financial statements, but also by the company's citizenship rating. In this kind of atmosphere, product quality, service delivery, and customer satisfaction take on even more meaning. Not only are they competitive tools, but they also become regulatory issues.

A company's financial health has long been measured and reported according to Generally Accepted Accounting Principles (GAAP). Everybody depends upon this system of accounting guidelines to track a company's performance, determine its tax liabilities, and evaluate its net worth. Now the time has come for a similar system that would formalize and standardize the measuring and reporting of companies' customer satisfaction levels. In addition to GAAP, we need a set of *Generally Accepted Service Principles*—GASP^{TM}.

Employing both in-house and independent service auditors, a company would use GASP to grade itself on service delivery and customer satisfaction, and the results would be reported regularly to all of the company's constituencies, including board members, shareholders, creditors, stock analysts, securities firms, the media, employees, and even customers. Much like financial data, GASP analyses would become a standard part of a company's quarterly and annual reports. Good or bad, they might also be posted in company offices, factories, warehouses, or other facilities for the benefit of employees; and when they're especially good, most companies would want to display them in stores for customers to see, or publicize them through advertisements, media releases, and mass mailings. It's vitally important, however, that GASP be taken every bit as seriously as accounting principles are. It should not be viewed simply as a public relations gimmick to be used whenever the results are favorable. For determining a company's *real* customer satisfaction index, GASP should become as professionally respected and reliable as GAAP is in determining financial status.

Exactly what kinds of things would GASP measure? The answer is: a company's entire delivery chain. All activities and attributes that affect customer satisfaction in a given industry would come under GASP inspection. Depending upon the type of business, that would include just about everything discussed in this book—and then some. For example, what is the company's customer churn rate? How many complaints were received last quarter compared to the quarter before or the same quarter a year ago? Are warranty claims increasing or decreasing? How much time do customers wait in line on average, and is waiting time dropping or rising? Assuming that a company periodically surveys its employees about service matters, what is the trend in employee complaints, suggestions, and attitudes toward service? And if a company routinely, or even occasionally, asks its customers to comment on service, what are the customers saying, and how do their responses compare to those of last month, last quarter, or last year?

Following is an example of how the Rainier Bancorporation of Seattle, Washington, tells its shareholders about customer perceptions of the bank's service (Figure 5–2). This "Service Quality" analysis is taken from Rainier's 1987 annual report, where it was accompanied by two full pages of detailed discussion about service quality. With a GASP system in place, any public corporation would be remiss if it didn't publish similar or even more extensive quality analyses in its annual reports.

By following a GASP system, companies will force themselves into a mode of regular, ongoing measurement and analysis of service delivery. GASP will provide concrete documentation and reveal trends that management

FIGURE 5–2.

Service Quality: How We Measure Up in Customer's Eye

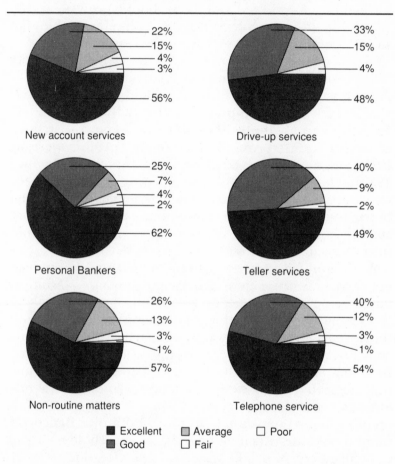

New account services — 22%, 15%, 4%, 3%, 56%

Drive-up services — 33%, 15%, 4%, 48%

Personal Bankers — 25%, 7%, 4%, 2%, 62%

Teller services — 40%, 9%, 2%, 49%

Non-routine matters — 26%, 13%, 3%, 1%, 57%

Telephone service — 40%, 12%, 3%, 1%, 54%

■ Excellent   ▨ Average   □ Poor
■ Good   □ Fair

needs to know about in order to pursue a strategy of continuous improvement. With a formal system such as this—one that everybody else uses and that has public recognition—it will be hard for managers to delude themselves or lie to others. The evidence will be right there for everybody to see, and there will be little room for excuses. In the same way companies explain good and bad trends in sales and profits, they would also explain upward or downward trends in service quality. Even with privately or closely held companies, where public disclosure is not required, the owners, managers, or potential partners and buy-out prospects should want to have a reliable, verifiable picture of any company's customer-satisfaction index.

A Moving Target

Jack Germain, retired senior vice president and director of quality for Motorola, says that total customer satisfaction is "a constantly moving target." Speaking in April, 1989 at the "Quest for Excellence" conference in Washington, D.C. , Germain said: "As our performance—and that of our competitors—improves, customer expectations will surely rise. Therefore, *continuous* improvement is absolutely essential."

Again and again when we read or hear what the leaders of the quality revolution are saying, we're confronted with the words "continuous," "ongoing," and "total." To those who have broken new ground and experienced both the challenges and rewards of improving customer satisfaction, there can be no compromises; it's all or nothing. In early 1987, Motorola's long-range quality goal was to improve product and services quality 10 times by 1989 and at least 100-fold by 1991. But even a 100-fold improvement in four years is not enough for Motorola. The company is dedicated to reaching what it calls "Six Sigma Capability" by 1992. Six Sigma represents what chairman Robert Galvin defines as "virtual perfection." It means *having only 3.4 defective parts out of every one million produced*. As John Marous of Westinghouse put it, "Ivory Soap used to be advertised back in the 1950s and 1960s as 'ninety-nine and forty-four one-hundredth's percent pure'—but getting things only ninety-nine-and-a-half percent right is no longer acceptable. The goal should be 100 percent."

The "just say no" slogan that is used today to combat drug abuse might well be borrowed by business and industry to combat low quality and poor service. That, in effect, is what CEO Arden Sims of Globe Metallurgical did in 1985. As Sims recounts: "We refused to accept the gloom spreading over America's smokestack industries. We refused to be swamped by a flood of cheap, imported commodity-grade metals. Other companies in our business closed their doors. But at Globe we raised our sights. We aimed at becoming the lowest-cost, highest-quality producer in the world . . . and we hit that mark. Now, when many European traders place orders, they specify 'Globe quality' no matter who the supplier is."

That's a very inspiring story, especially since it relates to such a small company that won against enormous odds. Of course, it took more than inspiration. It took intelligent, hard work and a willingness to face risks. But it started with an emotional dedication. As Corning's James Houghton says, "Total quality carries a spirit and a fervor of its own."

Any company that wants to survive and prosper today *has* to say "no" to bad quality and slipshod customer service. If it doesn't, then it will soon hear a rising chorus of "no's" from its customers. Paul Hawken, author of *The Next Economy*, wrote in a 1987 edition of the magazine *Marketing Communications* that companies should realize Americans are becoming more intelligent. "Companies that try to fool their customers or manipulate their employees will find themselves, sooner or later, competitively threatened by a company that does no such thing," Hawken warns us. He adds that companies that expect to do well will have to treat customers as they themselves want to be treated. "Consumers," he says, "are tired of two things: being treated as subordinates to a company, store, or institution and being seen as anonymous." James Houghton pursues this same theme when he says that success depends upon "constant interaction with customers — observing, listening, talking." And James I. Lader, a New York-based corporate communications consultant, wrote in the Summer 1988 issue of *The Quality Review* that "a company must instill a human-to-human sense of quality. It cannot rely simply on the physical or technological attributes of its products and services." Putting the human factor back into an American business environment that has become highly oriented to automation and dependent upon the quick fix is a hard order to fill, and the push-button solutions that have been in vogue for a number of years simply won't do. Some commentators, including *Fortune* magazine, have said that companies have to get the quality or service "religion." John J. Creedon, president of Metropolitan Life, uses the term "obsession" when he talks of service. "You really have to get your employees obsessed with the idea of wanting to be the best, or wanting to do things better, or improving quality constantly," advises Creedon. And from a manufacturer's point of view, Harold R. Tuten, vice president for operations at Globe Metallurgical, says, "The commitment to quality is more than statistics to the guy jockeying a charging buggy around the plant . . . it's a minute-to-minute reality."

Whether we characterize it as a "religion," "obsession," or with any other stirring imagery, the relatively recent reawakening to the importance of quality, service, and customer satisfaction has released a force that is gaining unstoppable momentum. Improving quality and service is an absolute necessity not only because customers demand it but also because America's economy cannot withstand foreign competition without it. You don't have to be in a business that competes head-on with Japan, Korea, Germany, or Italy to be affected by this imperative; as American consumers and business buyers get more accustomed to better quality no matter what its source, they will spurn the companies and products that don't deliver on a comparable level. And if you think you can crack the quality nut with a single blow and then sit back and enjoy the sweet meat, think *again* because your competitors—domestic or foreign—will be shaking the tree for more nuts. Mead D'Amore, general manager of the Westinghouse Nuclear Fuels Division, says that "what counts—to our customers, to our corporation, and to ourselves—is not what we have achieved in the past, but what we *can* accomplish tomorrow." Those are the words of a man who helped lead his company to win one of the first three Baldrige Awards, and what he's saying echoes what the other quality leaders are saying: We have only begun, and we intend to stay at it because real quality and superior service will be in demand from now on. America's age of mediocrity is fast becoming history.

1990 Application Guidelines

Malcolm Baldrige National Quality Award

"The improvement
of quality in
products and the
improvement of
quality in service –
these are national
priorities as
never before."

George Bush

*"The success of
the Malcolm Baldrige
National Quality Award
has demonstrated
that government and
industry, working together,
can foster excellence."*

Robert Mosbacher
Secretary of Commerce

Managed by:

United States Department of Commerce
National Institute of Standards and Technology
Gaithersburg, MD 20899
Telephone (301) 975-2036
Telefax (301) 948-3716

Administered by:
The Malcolm Baldrige National Quality
Award Consortium, Inc.

P.O. Box 443
Milwaukee, WI 53201-0443
Telephone (414) 272-8575
Telefax (414) 272-1734

P.O. Box 56606, Dept. 698
Houston, TX 77256-6606
Telephone (713) 681-4020
Telefax (713) 681-8578

THE MALCOLM BALDRIGE NATIONAL QUALITY IMPROVEMENT ACT OF 1987 – PUBLIC LAW 100-107

The Malcolm Baldrige National Quality Award was created by Public Law 100-107, signed into law on August 20, 1987. The Award Program, responsive to the purposes of Public Law 100-107, led to the creation of a new public-private partnership. Principal support for the program comes from the Foundation for the Malcolm Baldrige National Quality Award, established in 1988.

The Award is named for Malcolm Baldrige, who served as Secretary of Commerce from 1981 until his tragic death in a rodeo accident in 1987. His managerial excellence contributed to long-term improvement in efficiency and effectiveness of government.

The Findings and Purposes Section of Public Law 100-107 states that:

" 1. the leadership of the United States in product and process quality has been challenged strongly (and sometimes successfully) by foreign competition, and our Nation's productivity growth has improved less than our competitors over the last two decades.

2. American business and industry are beginning to understand that poor quality costs companies as much as 20 percent of sales revenues nationally, and that improved quality of goods and services goes hand in hand with improved productivity, lower costs, and increased profitability.

3. strategic planning for quality and quality imrovement programs, through a commitment to excellence in manufacturing and services, are becoming more and more essential to the well-being of our Nation's economy and our ability to compete effectively in the global marketplace.

4. improved management understanding of the factory floor, worker involvement in quality, and greater emphasis on statistical process control can lead to dramatic improvements in the cost and quality of manufactured products.

5. the concept of quality improvement is directly applicable to small companies as well as large, to service industries as well as manufacturing, and to the public sector as well as private enterprise.

6. in order to be successful, quality improvement programs must be management-led and customer-oriented and this may require fundamental changes in the way companies and agencies do business.

7. several major industrial nations have successfully coupled rigorous private sector quality audits with national awards giving special recognition to those enterprises the audits identify as the very best; and

8. a national quality award program of this kind in the United States would help improve quality and productivity by:

   A. helping to stimulate American companies to improve quality and productivity for the pride of recognition while obtaining a competitive edge through increased profits;

   B. recognizing the achievements of those companies which improve the quality of their goods and services and providing an example to others;

   C. establishing guidelines and criteria that can be used by business, industrial, governmental, and other organizations in evaluating their own quality improvement efforts, and

   D. providing specific guidance for other American organizations that wish to learn how to manage for high quality by making available detailed information on how winning organizations were able to change their cultures and achieve eminence."

```
07    834.01.01.10   04/10/92 12.30 2E
B.DALTON BOOKSELLER         DAYTON, C

0808150553                         2.9
          10 PCT. MARKDOWN         0.2

0808150596                         3.9
          10 PCT. MARKDOWN         0.3
0808150596                         3.9
          10 PCT. MARKDOWN         0.3
0808144332                         4.9
          10 PCT. MARKDOWN         0.4
0808144332                         4.9
          10 PCT. MARKDOWN         0.4
0808144332                         4.9
          10 PCT. MARKDOWN         0.4
                    SUBTOTAL      23.3
                    SALES TAX      1.5
                    TOTAL         24.8
6011005764000942 DISCOVER         24.8
       TOTAL SAVINGS    $2.54

--------------THANK YOU--------------
```

TABLE OF CONTENTS

"This Award offers a unique mechanism for cooperation between business leaders and quality experts throughout the private sector and government..."

Robert Mosbacher
Secretary of Commerce

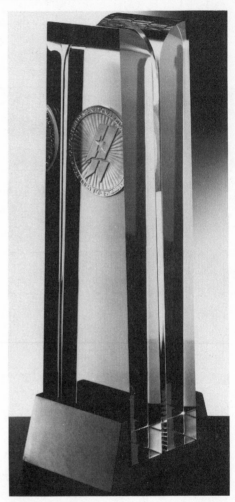

The Award is a three-part solid crystal stele standing 14 inches tall. An 18 karat gold plated medal is embedded in its central form. The medal bears the inscriptions: "Malcolm Baldrige National Quality Award" and "The Quest for Excellence" on one side and the Presidential seal on the other side.

Awards in 1988 and 1989 were presented by the President of the United States at special ceremonies in Washington D.C.

Award recipients may publicize and advertise receipt of the Award and will receive recognition for sharing information about their successful quality strategies.

Crystal by Steuben Glass
Medal by Medallic Art

NTRODUCTION

The Malcolm Baldrige National Quality Award is an annual Award to recognize U.S. companies which excel in quality achievement and quality management.

The Award promotes:

- awareness of quality as an increasingly important element in competitiveness,
- understanding of the requirements for quality excellence, and
- sharing of information on successful quality strategies and on the benefits derived from implementation of these strategies.

Companies participating in the Award process submit applications which include completion of the Award Examination. The Award Examination is based upon quality excellence criteria, created through a business-government partnership. In responding to these criteria, applicants are expected to provide information and data on their quality processes and quality improvement. Information and data submitted must be adequate to demonstrate that the applicant's approaches could be replicated or adapted by other businesses.

The Award Examination is designed to serve not only as a reliable basis for making Awards but also to permit a diagnosis of the applicant's overall quality management. All Award applicants receive feedback reports prepared by teams of U.S. quality experts.

EXECUTIVE SUMMARY

Eligibility

The Malcolm Baldrige National Quality Award recognizes U.S. companies which have attained a high level of quality excellence and thereby competitive advantage in domestic and world marketplaces. Eligibility for the Award is intended to be as open as possible to all U.S. companies. Any FOR-PROFIT business or appropriate subsidiary located in the United States may apply for an Award. Minor eligibility restrictions and conditions ensure fairness and consistency in definition.

Award Categories

1. Manufacturing companies or subsidiaries
2. Service companies or subsidiaries
3. Small businesses

Numbers of Awards

Up to two Awards may be given each year in each of three award categories. Fewer than two Awards may be given in a category if the high standards of the Award are not met.

1990 Award Schedule

- **Application Package** due April 25 (contents itemized below)
- **Review and Evaluation** – May through August
- **Site Visits** – August through September
- **Award Ceremony** – October or November

Applicants Need to Provide

1. **Eligibility Determination Form** — organizational information sufficient to determine eligibility prior to the application due date
2. **Application Package** – total contents of Award Application including:
    A. **Eligibility Determination Form** – with official eligibility confirmation
    B. **Application Form** – general descriptive information about the company
    C. **Site Listing and Descriptors Form** – information about the company's location and activities
    D. **Application Report** – responses to the 33 Award Examination Items.
       - Manufacturing and Service Company Application Reports are limited to 75 pages. Supplemental sections are required for certain Applicants.

       - Small Business Application Reports are limited to 50 pages; no Supplemental sections are required.

Feedback Reports

All applicants receive Feedback Reports summarizing their strengths, areas for improvement, and overall quality management profiles. Applicants in the 1988 and 1989 Award processes are using their feedback reports to strengthen their quality systems and practices.

Responsibilities of Award Recipients

Recipients receive visibility and recognition resulting from the Award. In addition to publicizing receipt of the Award, recipients are expected to share information about their successful quality strategies with other U.S. organizations.

Fees

Fees are set to cover some of the costs of review. A fee of $2,500 is charged for review of the basic written examination for the manufacturing and service categories. A fee of $1,000 is charged for the small business category. More detailed written examinations — required of organizations which need to describe multi-business or multi-product quality systems — result in proportionately higher fees. Separate site visit fees are set at the time site visits are scheduled.

Program Funding

Applicants are reviewed and site visits conducted without funding from the United States Government. Review expenses are paid primarily through application fees; partial support for the reviews is provided by the Foundation for the Malcolm Baldrige National Quality Award. Through extensive volunteer efforts and only modest compensation for some members of the Board of Examiners, application review and site visit fees are kept to a minimum.

Confidentiality

Individual applications, commentary, and scoring information developed during the review of applications are regarded as proprietary and are kept confidential. Such information is available only to those individuals directly involved in the evaluation and application distribution processes. Board of Examiner members are assigned to applications following strict conflict of interest rules and receive no information regarding the content or status of applications to which they are not assigned (see BOARD of EXAMINERS).

- Information on successful strategies of Award recipients *may be released only with written approval* of the recipients.

Summary of Changes from 1989 Requirements

- Companies planning to apply for the Award in 1990 are required to receive eligibility approval prior to submitting their applications.

- The application fee for manufacturing and service companies has been increased from $2000 to $2500.

- The application fee for small businesses has been decreased from $1200 to $1000.

- Site visit fees for small businesses have been reduced to one-half of those for companies in the manufacturing and service categories.

- Applicants need to describe significant quality management activities conducted in their foreign operations.

Malcolm Baldrige National Quality Award Board of Examiners

Members of the Malcolm Baldrige National Quality Award Board of Examiners review and evaluate all applications. The Board is comprised of approximately 150 quality experts selected from business, professional and trade organizations, accrediting bodies, universities and government. Selected each winter through an application process, Board of Examiner members meet the highest standards of qualification and peer recognition.

Board appointments are of three types: Examiners, Senior Examiners, and Judges. All members of the Board take part in an examination preparation course designed to ensure understanding, consistency and fairness throughout the examination process. The course addresses the intent of the examination items, the application of the scoring system, the preparation of feedback reports and the details of the examination process.

When assigning Board members to review applications, business and quality expertise are matched to the business of the applicant. Accordingly, applications from manufacturing companies are assigned primarily to Board members with manufacturing expertise, and service company applications are assigned primarily to those with service expertise.

Confidentiality
Board member assignments follow strict rules regarding real and potential conflict of interest. Board members sign agreements to abide by a Code of Ethics which includes non-disclosure of information from applications.

ELIGIBILITY CATEGORIES AND RESTRICTIONS

Basic Eligibility

Public Law 100-107 establishes the three eligibility categories of the Award: Manufacturing, Service and Small Business (described below). Any for-profit business located in the United States or its territories may apply for the Award. For example, publicly or privately-owned, domestic or foreign-owned, joint ventures, incorporated firms, sole proprietorships, partnerships, and holding companies may apply. Not eligible are: local, state and national government agencies, not-for-profit organizations, trade associations and professional societies.

Award Eligibility Categories

1. Manufacturing

Companies or subsidiaries (business units, divisions or like organizations) that produce and sell manufactured products or manufacturing processes and those companies which produce agricultural, mining, or construction products *(see SIC Codes 01-39)*.

2. Service

Companies or subsidiaries (business units, divisions or like organizations) that sell services *(see SIC Codes 40-89)*.

- Proper SIC Classification of companies that perform both manufacturing and service is determined by the larger percentage of sales.

3. Small Business

Complete businesses with not more than 500 full-time employees. Business activities may include manufacturing and/or service. The small business must be able to document that it functions independently of any equity owners.

Subsidiaries

In the Manufacturing and Service categories, subsidiaries, business units, and divisions or like components of a company may be eligible for the Award. Small businesses must apply as a whole; subsidiaries, business units, divisions or like components of small businesses are not eligible for an Award. For purposes of the Malcolm Baldrige National Quality Award application, the word subsidiary will be used to mean subsidiary, business unit, divisions or like components.

The following application conditions apply for subsidiaries:

- The subsidiary must have existed one year prior to the Award application;
- The subsidiary must have clear definition of organization as reflected in corporate literature, e.g., organization charts, administrative manuals, annual reports;
- The subsidiary must have more than 500 full-time employees OR
- it must have 20% of all employees in the world-wide operations of the parent company.

Note: The application of a subsidiary, business unit, division or like organization should describe the quality system for the full range of activities of a complete enterprise.

Restrictions on Eligibility

The intent of Public Law 100-107 is to create an Award process incorporating rigorous and objective evaluation of the applicants' total quality systems and underlying products and services. Award recipients are to serve as appropriate models of total quality achievement for other United States companies. Customer satisfaction is to play a major role in the examination. Site visits are required to verify descriptions given in written applications.

The nature of some companies' activities are such that the central purposes and requirements of Public Law 100-107 cannot be fulfilled through their participation in the Award program; companies or subsidiaries whose businesses cannot fulfill these purposes are not eligible. Specifically, three restrictions apply:

1. A company or its subsidiary is eligible only if the quality practices associated with all major business functions of the applicant are inspectable in the U.S. or its territories: One or more of the following three conditions must apply:

   - more than 50% of the applicant's employees must be located in the U.S. or its territories, or

   - more than 50% of the applicant's physical assets must be located in the U.S. or its territories, or

   - more than 50% of the total quality management operations which underlie the products and services it delivers are conducted inside the U.S. or its territories

   Note: The functions/activities of foreign sites must be included in the application report in the appropriate Examination Item.

2. For a subsidiary to be eligible, at least 50% of the customer base (dollar volume for products and services) must be free of direct financial and line organization control by the parent company. For example, a subsidiary is not eligible if its parent company or other subsidiary of the parent company are the customers for more than one-half of its total products and services.

3. Individual units or partial aggregations of units of "chain" organizations (such as hotels, retail stores, banks, or restaurants), where each unit performs a similar function, or manufactures a similar product, are not eligible.

Multiple-Application Restrictions

1. A subsidiary and its parent company may not both apply for Awards in the same year.

2. Only one subsidiary of a company may apply for an Award in the same year in the same Award category.

Future Eligibility Restrictions on Award Recipients

1. If a company receives an Award, the company and all its subsidiaries are ineligible to apply for another Award for a period of five years.

2. If a subsidiary receives an Award, it is ineligible to apply for another Award for a period of five years.

3. If a subsidiary constituting of more than one-half of the total sales of a company receives an Award, neither that company nor any of its other subsidiaries is eligible to apply for another Award for a period of five years.

TIMELINE AND APPLICATION REVIEW PROCESS

Eligibility Determination
February-April

↓

Applications
Due **April 25, 1990**

↓

Written Application
Review **May-August**

↓

Site Visits
August-September

↓

Award Ceremony
October or November

↓

Feedback Reports
Distributed
November-December

Eligibility Determination

Applicants must submit the *Eligibility Determination Form* (on page 9) prior to submitting an application. Within 14 days of receipt of the *Eligibility Descriptor Form* applicants will be notified of their eligibility status.

Applications must be postmarked or consigned to an   overnight mail delivery service by April 25, 1990 to be eligible for the 1990 Awards.

Application Review Process

Applications are reviewed by the Board of Examiners in a four-stage process:

1. First-Stage Review:

A review of the Application Report is conducted by at least four members of the Board of Examiners and led by a Senior Examiner. At the conclusion of the first-stage review, the Panel of Judges determines which applications should be referred for consensus review.

2. Consensus Review:

A review of the Application Report is conducted by at least four members of the Board of Examiners and led by a Senior Examiner. At the conclusion of the consensus review, the Panel of Judges determines which applicants should receive site visits.

A wide margin of safety is built into the decisions made at the conclusion of the first-stage review and at the conclusion of the consensus review to ensure that all applicants receive every reasonable consideration to advance to the next stage. The Judges consider applications case by case, and review scoring and scoring profiles. Each Award category — manufacturing, service, and small business — is considered separately. Strict conflict of interest rules apply and are carefully monitored at all four stages of review.

3. Site Visit Review

An on-site verification of the Application Report is conducted by at least five members of the Board of Examiners and led by a Senior Examiner. The site visit review team develops a report to the Panel of Judges.

The highest scoring candidates for the Award undergo site visits by members of the Board of Examiners. The primary objectives of the site visits are to verify the information provided in the Application Report and to clarify issues and questions raised during review of the Report. A site visit plan is cooperatively developed by the applicant and the site visit team. A site visit agenda is provided to the company at least two weeks in advance of the visit. The site visit agenda includes, but is not limited to, a schedule of planned visits to the applicant's facilities and operating units, a list of corporate officials to be interviewed, an estimate of time requirements for the visits, and the names of Examiners scheduled to participate. Site visits consist primarily of the conduct of interviews by Examiner teams and their review of pertinent records and data. Applicants are asked to make introductory and concluding presentations.

4. Judges' Final Review

A final review of all evaluation reports is conducted by the Panel of Judges to recommend Award recipients. The Panel of Judges develops a set of recommendations made to the National Institute of Standards and Technology. The Institute presents the Judges' recommendations to the Secretary of Commerce for Award decisions.

Awards in 1988 and 1989 were presented by the President of the United States in special ceremonies in Washington, D.C.

All applicants receive Feedback Reports at the close of the Award cycle.

SCORING SYSTEM

The system for scoring Examination Items is based upon three evaluation dimensions: (1) approach; (2) deployment; and (3) results. All Examination Items require applicants to furnish information relating to one or more of these dimensions. Specific criteria associated with the evaluation dimensions are described below.

Approach

Approach refers to the methods the company uses to achieve the purposes addressed in the Examination Items. The scoring criteria used to evaluate approaches include one or more of the following:

- the degree to which the approach is prevention based
- the appropriateness of the tools, techniques, and methods to the requirements
- the effectiveness of the use of tools, techniques, and methods
- the degree to which the approach is systematic, integrated, and consistently applied
- the degree to which the approach embodies effective self-evaluation, feedback, and adaptation cycles to sustain continuous improvement
- the degree to which the approach is based upon quantitative information that is objective and reliable
- the indicators of unique and innovative approaches, including significant and effective new adaptations of tools and techniques used in other applications or types of businesses

Deployment

Deployment refers to the extent to which the approaches are applied to all relevant areas and activities addressed and implied in the Examination Items. The scoring criteria used to evaluate deployment include one or more of the following:

- the appropriate and effective application to all product and service characteristics
- the appropriate and effective application to all transactions and interactions with customers, suppliers of goods and services, and the public
- the appropriate and effective application to all internal processes, activities, facilities, and employees

Results

Results refers to *outcomes* and *effects* in achieving the purposes addressed and implied in the Examination Items. The scoring criteria used to evaluate results include one or more of the following:

- the quality levels demonstrated
- the contributions of the outcomes and effects to quality improvement
- the rate of quality improvement
- the breadth of quality improvement
- the demonstration of sustained improvement
- the significance of improvements to the company's business
- the comparison with industry and world leaders
- the company's ability to show that improvements derive from their quality practices and actions

BUSINESS FACTORS CONSIDERED IN THE EVALUATION OF APPLICATIONS

The Award Examination is designed to permit evaluation of the widest range of quality systems for manufacturing and service companies of any size, type of business, or scope of market. The 33 Items and 133 Areas to Address have been selected because of their importance to virtually all businesses. Nevertheless, the importance of the Items and Areas to Address may not be equally applicable to all businesses, even to businesses of comparable size in the same industry. Specific business factors that may bear upon the evaluation are considered at every stage of preparation for evaluations as well as in the evaluations themselves. Below is an outline of the key business factors considered and how they are addressed in the Award Program.

Key Business Factors

- size and resources of the applicant
- nature of the applicant's business: products, services, and technologies
- scope of the applicant's market: local, regional, national or international
- regulatory environment within which the applicant operates
- importance of suppliers, dealers, and other external businesses to the applicant and the degree of influence the applicant has over its suppliers

How Business Factors are Considered in the Award Processes

- Appointments to the Board of Examiners are made to create a Board with a range of expertise, covering both manufacturing and service businesses.
- All Board members take part in a preparation course that includes instructions on how key business factors should be taken into account in evaluations. The preparation course includes study materials on manufacturing and service companies.
- Assignments of Board members to applications are made to provide the best matches between Examiners' experience and the businesses of the applicants.
- Applicants provide information on the key factors that affect their businesses in overviews reviewed by all Board members assigned to the applications.
- Applicants do not lose credit in evaluations if one or more of the Areas to Address does not pertain to their businesses or quality systems.

- All applications receive multiple evaluations. The Panel of Judges considers all scores, scoring profiles, and details of strengths and areas for improvement at all stages of their review.
- Wide margins of safety are built into decisions made by the Panel of Judges at three key stages: (1) after the first-stage review; (2) after the consensus review; and (3) after initial review of site visit reports. The judging procedures ensure that applicants are not eliminated based upon small differences in scoring.
- Judges' decisions at every stage are made on a category-by-category (manufacturing, service and small business) basis. This ensures that comparisons take place among applicants in similar businesses.

Below is a summary by Examination Category of how key business factors are taken into account in evaluation.

Leadership

This Category examines the senior executives' leadership in creating quality values, building the values into the way the company does business, and how the executives and the company project the quality values outside the company. Participation in activities such as those of national and international organizations and other activities given in this Category depends upon the type and resources of the business, and its overall competitive and regulatory environments. Evaluations are based upon the appropriateness, effectiveness, and extent of the executives' and of the company's involvement in relation to the size and type of business. Whether or not the company has a quality department or officer, or regulatory affairs office or officer are not considered in the evaluation.

Information and Analysis

This Category examines the scope, validity, and use of data to determine the adequacy of the data system to support total quality management. The scope, management, and analysis of data depend upon the type of business, its resources, number and geographical distribution of business units, and other factors. Evaluations are based upon the appropriateness and effectiveness of methods for management of data, information and analysis and of technology in relation to these business factors. Evaluations do not depend upon how activities are organized or whether or not the company has an information department or officer, or uses particular technologies to analyze data or to make data available throughout the company.

Strategic Quality Planning

This Category examines the company's approach to planning to determine its adequacy to achieve or sustain quality leadership. While the planning processes and priority development do not depend appreciably upon the size and type of business, the scope and type of benchmark and competitive data may depend upon such business factors. Competitive and benchmark data are essential for planning quality leadership because they make possible clear and objective quality comparisons. The principal considerations in assessing the effectiveness of competitive and benchmark data are in relation to the competitive environment and resources of the company. However, if a company operates in a local or regional market, and there are other, non-competing companies in similar markets elsewhere, the company would be expected to reach beyond its local or regional market for competitive and benchmark data on key product, process, and service features.

Evaluations of planning are based upon the thoroughness and effectiveness of processes including the information used. Evaluations do not depend upon how planning activities are organized or whether or not the company has a planning department or officer.

Human Resource Utilization

This Category examines the company's efforts to develop and involve the entire work force in total quality. The organization of efforts to develop and involve employees depends upon the number of employees, resources of the company, the geographical distribution of business units and other factors. Evaluations depend upon the appropriateness and effectiveness of approaches to human resource development and do not depend upon whether or not the company has either a human resource department or officer, or training and education specialists or facilities. For example, education and training might be accomplished in a variety of ways such as through schools, contract, or through training given by customers.

Quality Assurance of Products and Services

This Category has a very strong process and systems orientation throughout. Processes may be carried out entirely by employees, largely by means of technology, or through a combination of the two. The degree of formality in systems and processes depends upon a number of factors such as size of the business, types of products and services, customer and government requirements, regulatory requirements, and number of business locations. Evaluations take into account consistency of execution of quality operations that incorporate a sound prevention basis accompanied by continuous quality improvement activities. Consistency of execution is taken to mean the existence of defined, suitably-recorded processes with clear delineation of responsibilities. Evaluations do not depend upon how responsibilities are distributed or organized or whether or not the company has a quality organization or officer. Moreover, in small businesses, one person might carry out two or more functions.

Quality Results

This Category examines the company's quality improvement and quality levels by themselves and in relation to those of competitors. Included are quality of products and services, internal operations, and suppliers. The number and type of measures depend upon factors such as the company's size, types of products and services, and competitive environment. Evaluations take such factors into account and consider whether or not the measures are sufficient to support overall improvement and to establish clear quality levels and comparisons.

Customer Satisfaction

This Category examines the company's knowledge of customer requirements, service and responsiveness, and satisfaction results measured through a variety of indicators. The scope and organization of activities to gather information, to serve and to respond to customers depend upon many factors such as company resources, types of products and services, and geographical distribution of business units and customers. Evaluations are based upon the appropriateness and effectiveness of efforts in relation to these business factors. They also take into account whether or not a company utilizes all instruments at its disposal or within its resources to meet all the key requirements of an excellent customer service system. Evaluations do not depend upon how responsibilities are distributed or whether or not the company has separate departments for customer service, complaints or other special purposes.

EXAMINATION CATEGORIES, ITEMS AND POINT VALUES
Malcolm Baldrige National Quality Award

1990 Examination Categories/Items	Maximum Points
1.0 Leadership	**100**
1.1 Senior Executive Leadership	30
1.2 Quality Values	20
1.3 Management for Quality	30
1.4 Public Responsibility	20
2.0 Information and Analysis	**60**
2.1 Scope and Management of Quality Data and Information	35
2.2 Analysis of Quality Data and Information	25
3.0 Strategic Quality Planning	**90**
3.1 Strategic Quality Planning Process	40
3.2 Quality Leadership Indicators in Planning	25
3.3 Quality Priorities	25
4.0 Human Resource Utilization	**150**
4.1 Human Resource Management	30
4.2 Employee Involvement	40
4.3 Quality Education and Training	40
4.4 Employee Recognition and Performance Measurement	20
4.5 Employee Well-Being and Morale	20
5.0 Quality Assurance of Products and Services	**150**
5.1 Design and Introduction of Quality Products and Services	30
5.2 Process and Quality Control	25
5.3 Continuous Improvement of Processes, Products and Services	25
5.4 Quality Assessment	15
5.5 Documentation	10
5.6 Quality Assurance, Quality Assessment and Quality Improvement of Support Services and Business Processes	25
5.7 Quality Assurance, Quality Assessment and Quality Improvement of Suppliers	20
6.0 Quality Results	**150**
6.1 Quality of Products and Services	50
6.2 Comparison of Quality Results	35
6.3 Business Process, Operational and Support Service Quality Improvement	35
6.4 Supplier Quality Improvement	30
7.0 Customer Satisfaction	**300**
7.1 Knowledge of Customer Requirements and Expectations	50
7.2 Customer Relationship Management	30
7.3 Customer Service Standards	20
7.4 Commitment to Customers	20
7.5 Complaint Resolution for Quality Improvement	30
7.6 Customer Satisfaction Determination	50
7.7 Customer Satisfaction Results	50
7.8 Customer Satisfaction Comparison	50
TOTAL POINTS	**1000**

1990 EXAMINATION

1.0 Leadership (100 pts.)

The *Leadership* category examines how the senior executives create and sustain a clear and visible quality value system along with a supporting management system to guide all activities of the company toward quality excellence. Also examined are the senior executives' and the company's quality leadership in the external community and how the company integrates its public responsibilities with its quality values and practices.

1.1 Senior Executive Leadership
(30 pts.)

Describe the senior executives' leadership, personal involvement and visibility in developing and maintaining an environment for quality excellence.

AREAS TO ADDRESS

a. senior executives' leadership and personal involvement in quality-related activities such as goal setting, planning, review of quality plans and progress, teams, giving and receiving education and training, recognition of employees, learning about the quality of domestic and international competitors, and meeting with customers and suppliers

b. senior executives' approach to building the quality values into the leadership process of the company

c. senior executives' communication, access and contact within the company

d. senior executives' leadership and communication of quality excellence outside the company to groups such as national, trade, business, professional and community organizations, and schools

Note: *The term* **senior executives** *refers to the highest ranking official of the organization applying for the Award and those reporting directly to that official.*

1.2 Quality Values *(20 pts.)*

Describe the company's quality values, how they are projected in a consistent manner, and how adoption of the values throughout the company is assessed and reinforced.

AREAS TO ADDRESS

a. brief summary of the content of policy, mission or guidelines that demonstrate the company's quality values

b. company's communications activities and plans to project the values throughout the company

c. recent or current actions that demonstrate the importance of the quality values with respect to other business considerations, such as short-term profits and schedules

d. how the company evaluates the extent to which the quality values have been adopted throughout the company, such as through surveys, interviews or other means, and how employee acceptance is reinforced

1.3 Management for Quality
30 pts.)

Describe how the company integrates its quality values into day-to-day management of all units.

AREAS TO ADDRESS

a. key strategies for involving all levels of management and supervision in quality, and principal roles and responsibilities at each level

b. key strategies to promote cooperation among managers and supervisors at all levels such as through use of interunit teams or internal customer/supplier techniques

c. types, frequency and content of company reviews of the status of quality plans, and types of actions taken to assist units not performing according to plans

d. how management assesses the effectiveness of its approaches and improves or changes its approaches to integrating quality values into day-to-day management

e. key indicators of involvement of all levels of management and of effective cooperation among managers

1.4 Public Responsibility *(20 pts.)*

Describe how the company extends its quality leadership to the external community and integrates its responsibilities to the public for health, safety, environmental protection, and ethical business practice into its quality policies and activities.

AREAS TO ADDRESS

a. promoting quality awareness and sharing with external groups such as community, business, trade, school and government organizations

b. encouraging employee leadership and involvement in quality activities of professional, local, state, national, trade, business and education groups and in industry, national and international standards activities

c. full integration of business ethics, public health and safety, environmental protection, waste management and other regulatory requirements into overall quality leadership policies, systems and continuous improvement objectives

2.0 Information and Analysis *(60 pts.)*

The *Information and Analysis* category examines the scope, validity, use, and management of data and information that underlie the company's total quality management system. Also examined is the adequacy of the data and information to support a responsive prevention approach to quality based upon "management by fact."

2.1 Scope and Management of Quality Data and Information *(35 pts.)*

Describe the company's base of data and information used for planning, management, and evaluation of quality, and how data and information reliability, timeliness, and access are assured.

AREAS TO ADDRESS

a. criteria for selecting items to be included in the quality-related data and information base

b. scope and types of data: customers; internal operations and processes; employee-related; safety, health and other regulatory; competitive and benchmark data; quality results; supplier quality; and other

c. processes and technologies the company uses to ensure validity, consistency, standardization, review, update and timely access throughout the company

Note: *The purpose of this Item is to permit the applicant to demonstrate the* breadth and depth *of the data assembled as part of its total quality management effort. Applicants should give brief descriptions of the types of data under major headings such as "employees" and subheadings such as "education and training," "teams," and "recognition." Under each subheading, give a brief description of the data and information. Actual data should not be reported in this Item. Such data are requested in other Examination Items.*

2.2 Analysis of Quality Data and Information *(25 pts.)*

Describe how data and information are analyzed to support the company's key quality leadership objectives in a timely manner.

AREAS TO ADDRESS

a. principal types of analysis performed such as determination of trends, projections of quality improvements that should result from changes in practice or technology, evaluation of the performance of key systems, and assessment of long-term performance of products

b. how analysis supports key objectives and functions such as planning, day-to-day quality improvement activities, policy development, human resource strategy development, and management review of quality

c. steps taken and plans to shorten the cycle of data gathering, analysis, and access to improve support of company quality objectives

d. how analysis leads to changes in types of data collected, improved reliability of data, and improved analytical capabilities

3.0 Strategic Quality Planning *(90 pts.)*

The **Strategic Quality Planning** category examines the company's planning process for retaining or achieving quality leadership and how the company integrates quality improvement planning into overall business planning. Also examined are the company's short-term and longer-term priorities to achieve and/or sustain a quality leadership position.

3.1 Strategic Quality Planning Process *(40 pts.)*

Describe the company's strategic quality planning process for short-term (1-2 years) and longer-term (3-5 years or more) quality leadership and customer satisfaction.

AREAS TO ADDRESS

a. how strategic quality plans are developed and how they are integrated with overall business planning

b. principal types of data, information and analysis used in planning and feasibility evaluation such as customer requirements, process capabilities, competitive and benchmark data, and supplier data

c. principal roles competitive and benchmark data play in determining projected or potential improvements in quality, closing quality gaps, or exceeding competitors' capabilities

d. how employees, suppliers, and customers contribute to planning

e. how key requirements such as new technology, employee education and training, and improvements in supplier quality are determined

f. how plans are implemented such as through priority initiatives or projects; how resources are committed for key requirements such as capital expenditures and training; and how specific requirements are deployed to all work units and to suppliers

g. how the planning process is evaluated and improved

3.2 Quality Leadership Indicators in Planning *(25 pts.)*

Describe the company's approach to selecting quality-related competitive comparisons and world-class benchmarks to support strategic quality planning.

AREAS TO ADDRESS

a. criteria the company uses for selecting competitive comparisons and benchmarks: what areas to benchmark and with whom to compare

b. current sources of competitive and benchmark data including company and independent testing

c. current actions and plans to change the scope of competitive and benchmark data, to seek new or additional sources of such data, or to change the basis for selection

3.3 Quality Priorities *(25 pts.)*

Summarize the company's principal quality priorities and plans for the short term (1-2 years) and longer term (3-5 years or more).

AREAS TO ADDRESS

a. principal short-term and longer-term priorities and their relationship to the company's leadership objectives

b. resources committed to plans for education and training, technology and other key requirements

c. how the company will ensure that suppliers are able to meet its quality requirements

d. projection of major changes in the company's competitive quality position based upon implementation of the plan

4.0 Human Resource Utilization *(150 pts.)*

The **Human Resource Utilization** category examines the effectiveness of the company's efforts to develop and realize the full potential of the work force, including management, and to maintain an environment conducive to full participation, quality leadership, and personal and organizational growth.

4.1 Human Resource Management *(30 pts.)*

Describe how the company's human resource plans support its quality leadership objectives; summarize principal short-term (1-2 years) and longer-term (3-5 years or more) priorities.

AREAS TO ADDRESS

a. how the company integrates its human resource plans with the quality requirements of business plans

b. key strategies for increasing the involvement, effectiveness and productivity of all categories of employees, including hourly, bargaining unit and contract employees, and managers

c. principal human resource priorities for the short term and longer term and how they relate to the company's quality priorities

d. how the company uses its overall employee-related data to evaluate and improve its human resource management, strategies, practices and plans

Note: *Key strategies might include one or more of the following: mechanisms for promoting cooperation such as internal customer/supplier techniques or other internal partnerships; initiatives to promote labor-management cooperation such as partnerships with unions; creation or modifications in recognition systems; mechanisms for increasing or broadening employee responsibilities; and education and training initiatives. They might also include developing partnerships with educational institutions to develop employees and to help ensure the future supply of well-prepared employees.*

4.2 Employee Involvement *(40 pts.)*

Describe the means available for all employees to contribute effectively to the company's quality objectives; summarize trends in involvement.

AREAS TO ADDRESS

a. approaches to group participation such as teams: within functional units; between functional units; and involving suppliers and customers

b. other opportunities for employees to contribute, such as through suggestion systems or hotlines, and how and when the company gives feedback

c. approaches to enhanced employee authority to act (empowerment) such as when quality standards may be compromised; means for encouraging employee innovation; and means for increasing employee responsibilities

d. trends in key indicators of involvement, empowerment, and innovation for all categories of employees

e. principal means the company uses to evaluate the extent and effectiveness of involvement of categories of employees

4.3 Quality Education and Training *(40 pts.)*

Describe how the company decides what quality education and training is needed by employees and how it utilizes the knowledge and skills acquired; summarize the types of quality education and training received by employees in all employee categories.

AREAS TO ADDRESS

a. approach and rationale for deciding what quality education and training, such as training in statistical and other quantitative problem solving methods, is needed by different categories of employees

b. how the company provides on-job reinforcement of the knowledge and skills acquired in education and training

c. summary and trends in types of quality education and training received by each employee category. The summary and trends may address quality orientation of new employees, percent of employees receiving education and training in each category, quality education and training costs per employee, and average hours of quality education and training annually per employee.

d. indicators of effectiveness of the company's education and training activities and how the indicators are used to improve these activities

4.4 Employee Recognition and Performance Measurement *(20 pts.)*

Describe how the company's recognition and performance measurement processes support quality improvement; summarize trends in recognition.

AREAS TO ADDRESS

a. key strategies for encouraging contributions to quality including recognition of individuals and groups; how balance is achieved — between individual and group recognition and between individual and group performance — to ensure effective support for company quality improvement efforts

b. how recognition and performance measures reinforce quality relative to other business considerations such as quantity; how employees are involved in the development of measures

c. summary and trends in recognition of individuals and groups, by employee category, for contributions to quality improvement

d. how the company evaluates the effectiveness of its recognition and performance measurement systems, including soliciting feedback from employees, to improve its strategies and methods

4.5 Employee Well-Being and Morale *(20 pts.)*

Describe how the company safeguards the health and safety of employees, ensures comfort and physical protection, and maintains a supportive work environment; summarize trends in employee well-being and morale.

AREAS TO ADDRESS

a. how well-being and morale factors such as health, safety, satisfaction, and ergonomics are included in quality improvement activities

b. analysis of underlying causes of accidents, work-related health problems, and dissatisfaction, for elimination of adverse conditions

c. mobility, flexibility and retraining in job assignments to support employee development and/or to accommodate changes in technology, improved productivity or changes in work processes

d. special services, facilities and opportunities the company makes available to support employees. These might include one or more of the following: counseling, assistance, recreational or cultural, and non-work-related education

e. how employee satisfaction is determined, evaluated and used in quality improvement

f. trends in key indicators of well-being and morale such as safety, absenteeism, turnover, satisfaction, grievances, strikes and worker compensation. Explain adverse indicators and how problems were resolved or current status. Compare most significant indicators with those of industry averages and industry leaders.

5.0 Quality Assurance of Products and Services *(150 pts.)*

The **Quality Assurance of Products and Services** category examines the systematic approaches used by the company for total quality control of goods and services based primarily upon process design and control, including control of procured materials, parts and services. Also examined is the integration of quality control with continuous quality improvement.

5.1 Design and Introduction of Quality Products and Services

(30 pts.)

Describe how new or improved products and services are designed and introduced to meet or exceed customer requirements and how processes are designed to deliver according to the requirements.

AREAS TO ADDRESS

a. conversion of customer needs and expectations into product and process requirements and/or service quality standards

b. methods and their application for assuring quality in the design, development and validation stages; methods of testing and evaluating products, processes, and services before introduction, including review of designs for feasibility and assessment of key factors in production and use

c. detailed control plan: (1) selecting and setting key process characteristics to be controlled and how they are to be controlled, and (2) service process and delivery plan including selection of key characteristics to be controlled and how they are to be controlled

d. steps taken in design to minimize introduction time

Notes: *(1) In responding to this Item, applicants should interpret product and service characteristics broadly. Most companies have both product and service characteristics to consider.*

(2) Depending on their type of business, applicants need to consider many factors in product and service design including health, safety, long-term performance, measurement capability, process capability, and supplier capability. Applicant responses should reflect the requirements of the products and services they deliver.

5.2 Process and Quality Control

(25 pts.)

Describe how the processes which produce the company's products and services are controlled and how the company assures that products and services meet design plans or specifications.

AREAS TO ADDRESS

a. principal approaches the company uses to ensure that processes which produce products and services are adequately controlled

b. principal approaches the company uses routinely to ensure that products and services meet design plans or specifications

c. method for assuring that measurement quality is adequate to evaluate products, processes and services within the limits established in control plans

d. principal approaches to identify root causes of process upsets

e. principal approaches to the design of the measures to correct process upsets, and methods of verifying that the measures produce the predicted results and are effectively utilized in all appropriate units of the company

f. principal approaches of the company to use the information obtained from process and quality control for prevention and quality improvement

Note: *For manufacturing and service companies with measurement requirements, it is necessary to demonstrate that measurement accuracy and precision meet process and product requirements (measurement quality assurance). For physical, chemical and engineering measurements, indicate approaches for ensuring that measurements are traceable to national standards through calibrations, reference materials or other means.*

5.3 Continuous Improvement of Processes, Products and Services *(25 pts.)*

Describe how products and services are continuously improved through optimization and improvement of processes.

AREAS TO ADDRESS

a. principal approaches to identify opportunities for continuous improvement of processes, including reductions in response times: evaluation of all process steps; development and assessment of alternative processes; evaluation of new or improved technology; use of competitive and benchmark data

b. methods of process optimization such as controlled experiments

c. method for verifying that improvements produce the predicted results

d. method of integrating continuous improvement with daily operations and routine process and quality control and of ensuring effective integration by all appropriate units of the company

5.4 Quality Assessment *(15 pts.)*

Describe how the company assesses the quality of products, processes, services and quality practices.

AREAS TO ADDRESS

a. principal approaches the company uses to assess quality, quality systems and quality practices such as systems audits, product audits and service audits. Briefly describe the approaches and how the validity of assessment tools is assured.

b. types and frequencies of assessments and who conducts them: the company, customers, government or other

c. how assessment findings are translated into improvements such as in processes, practices, training and supplier requirements

d. method for verifying that improvements are made and that they are producing the predicted results

5.5 Documentation *(10 pts.)*

Describe documentation and other modes of "knowledge preservation" and transfer to support quality assurance, assessment and improvement.

AREAS TO ADDRESS

a. documentation system supporting quality assurance, assessment and improvement; types of documents and types of activities covered; and how documents are used such as in standardization, orientation of new employees, and training

b. timely update to keep pace with changes in technology, practice and quality improvement; disposal of obsolete documents

c. company efforts to improve responsiveness and access of the documentation system such as through use of computers and networks

5.6 Quality Assurance, Quality Assessment and Quality Improvement of Support Services and Business Processes (25 pts.)

Describe how the quality of support services and business processes is assured, assessed and improved.

AREAS TO ADDRESS

a. how the quality of support services and business processes is assured such as through process and quality control and quality assessment; how and how often quality is assessed through audits, reviews or other means

b. how support services and business processes are continuously improved

c. current strategies, efforts and plans to increase and improve the participation of support services in quality activities

Notes: (1) Examples of support services might include finance and accounting, software services, sales, marketing, information services, purchasing, personnel, legal services, maintenance, plant and facilities management, research and development, and secretarial and other administrative services.

(2) The purpose of this Item is to permit applicants to highlight separately the quality assurance, quality assessment and quality improvement activities for functions that support the primary processes through which products and services are produced. Together, Items 5.1, 5.2, 5.3, 5.4, 5.5, 5.6 and 5.7 should cover all operations, processes and activities of all work units. However, the selection of support services and business processes for inclusion in this Item depends on the type of business and quality system, and should be made by the applicant.

5.7 Quality Assurance, Quality Assessment and Quality Improvement of Suppliers (20 pts.)

Describe how the quality of materials, components, and services furnished by other businesses is assured, assessed and improved.

AREAS TO ADDRESS

a. process used to assure that the company's quality requirements are being met by suppliers by means such as audits, inspections, certification and testing

b. strategy and current efforts to improve the quality and responsiveness of suppliers, such as through partnerships, training, incentives and recognition, and to improve supplier selection

Note: The term supplier refers to external providers of goods and services.

6.0 Quality Results (150 pts.)

The **Quality Results** category examines quality levels and quality improvement based upon objective measures derived from analysis of customer requirements and expectations and from analysis of business operations. Also examined are current quality levels in relation to those of competing firms.

6.1 Quality of Products and Services (50 pts.)

Summarize trends in quality improvement based upon key product and service quality measures derived from customer needs and expectations.

AREAS TO ADDRESS

a. summarize trends in key product and service quality measures

b. explain adverse trends and outline what steps the company has taken or plans to take to prevent recurrence

Note: Key product and service quality measures are the set of principal measurable characteristics of products and services, including delivery and after-sales services, which, taken together, best represent the factors that predict customer satisfaction and quality in customer use. Examples include measures of accuracy, reliability, timeliness, performance, behavior, delivery, documentation and appearance. Customer satisfaction or other customer data should not be included in responses to this Item.

2 Comparison of Quality Results *(35 pts.)*

Compare the company's current quality levels with industry averages, industry leaders and world leaders, based upon the key product and service quality measures reported in Item 6.1.

AREAS TO ADDRESS

a. bases for comparison such as independent reports, company evaluations, laboratory testing, and benchmarks

b. current quality level comparisons with industry averages, industry leaders, and world leaders or other competitors in the company's key markets

c. current levels and trends in relation to the company's quality leadership objectives and plans. Explain adverse trends.

3 Business Process, Operational and Support Service Quality Improvement *(35 pts.)*

Summarize trends in quality improvement, based upon key measures of business processes, operations and support services.

AREAS TO ADDRESS

a. trends in key operating quality measures for business processes, operations which produce the company's products and services, and support services

b. explain adverse trends and outline what steps the company has taken or plans to prevent recurrence

c. comparisons with industry averages, industry leaders and world leaders when such data are available. Briefly explain adverse indicators.

Note: *Key operating quality measures are the set of principal measurable characteristics of processes such as use of manpower, materials, energy and capital. Appropriate measures relate to lead times, yields, waste, inventory levels, rework of products and repeat of services, first-time success rates, environmental improvements, and other areas.*

4 Supplier Quality Improvement *(30 pts.)*

Summarize trends in improvement in quality of supplies and services furnished by other companies, based upon key measures of product and service quality.

AREAS TO ADDRESS

a. trends in key indicators of the quality of supplies and services. Briefly explain adverse trends.

b. brief explanation of current supplier quality and trends in terms of the company's key requirements and actions to improve supplier quality

c. highlight awards and recognition the company's key suppliers have received and the role the company played in helping suppliers improve their quality

7.0 Customer Satisfaction *(300 pts.)*

The **Customer Satisfaction** category examines the company's knowledge of the customer, overall customer service systems, responsiveness, and its ability to meet requirements and expectations. Also examined are current levels and trends in customer satisfaction.

7.1 Knowledge of Customer Requirements and Expectations *(50 pts.)*

Describe how the company determines current and future customer requirements and expectations.

AREAS TO ADDRESS

a. process for identifying market segments, customer and potential customer groups, including customers of competitors, and their requirements and expectations through surveys, interviews and other contacts. (Include information on frequency, duration, objectivity, and depth of data collection and who collects such information.)

b. process for identifying product and service quality features and the relative importance of these features to customers or customer groups

c. cross comparisons with other key data and information such as complaints, losses and gains of customers, and performance data that may yield information on customer requirements and expectations and on key product and service features

d. how the company evaluates and improves the effectiveness of its processes for determining customer requirements and expectations such as improved surveys, other customer contacts, analysis, or cross comparisons

Notes: *(1) The buyer of a product or service may not be the end user. Thus, identifying customer groups needs to take into account both the buyer and the end user.*

(2) Product and service features refer to all important characteristics experienced by the customers, including delivery and after-sales service, that may bear upon customer preference and customer view of quality. These features also include the overall purchase and ownership experiences.

7.2 Customer Relationship Management *(30 pts.)*

Describe how the company provides effective management of its relationships with customers and how it ensures continuous improvement of customer relationship management.

AREAS TO ADDRESS

a. process for ensuring that customer service requirements are understood and responded to throughout the company

b. means for ensuring easy access for customers to comment, seek assistance, and complain

c. follow-up with customers on products and services to determine satisfaction and to gain information for improvement

d. empowering customer-contact employees to resolve problems promptly and to take extraordinary measures when appropriate

e. special hiring requirements, attitudinal and other training, recognition, and attitude/morale determination of customer-contact employees

f. technology and logistics (infrastructure) support to enable customer-contact employees to provide effective and timely customer service

g. analysis of complaint information, gains and losses of customers, and lost orders to assess costs and market consequences for policy review

h. process for evaluating and improving services to customers

3 Customer Service Standards *(20 pts.)*

Describe the company's standards governing the direct contact between employees and customers, and how these standards are set and modified.

AREAS TO ADDRESS

a. selection of well-defined, objectively-measurable standards derived from customer requirements and expectations

b. employee involvement in developing, evaluating and improving or changing standards

c. deployment of requirements and/or standards information to all company units to ensure effective support for customer-contact employees who are expected to meet the company's customer-service standards

d. tracking to ensure that key service standards are met

e. how service standards are evaluated and improved

4 Commitment to Customers *(20 pts.)*

Describe the company's commitments to customers on its explicit and implicit promises underlying its products and services.

AREAS TO ADDRESS

a. product and service guarantees and product warranties: comprehensiveness, conditions, understandability and credibility

b. other types of commitments the company makes to promote trust and confidence in its products and services

c. how improvements in the company's products and/or services over the past three years have been translated into changes in guarantees, warranties and other commitments

5 Complaint Resolution for Quality Improvement *(30 pts.)*

Describe how the company handles complaints, resolves them, and uses complaint information for quality improvement and prevention of recurrence of problems.

AREAS TO ADDRESS

a. process for ensuring that formal and informal complaints and critical comments made to different company units are aggregated for overall evaluation and use wherever appropriate throughout the company

b. process for ensuring that complaints are resolved promptly by customer-contact employees; summarize indicators of improved response including trends in response time

c. process for analyzing complaints to determine underlying causes and using this information to make improvements such as in processes, standards, and information to customers

d. process for evaluating the company's handling of complaints to improve both the response to complaints and the ability to translate the findings into preventive measures

7.6 Customer Satisfaction Determination *(50 pts.)*

Describe the company's methods for determining customer satisfaction, how this information is used in quality improvement, and how methods for determining customer satisfaction are improved.

AREAS TO ADDRESS

a. types and frequency of methods used including procedures to ensure objectivity and validity

b. how satisfaction is segmented by customer groups, if appropriate, and how satisfaction relative to competitors is determined

c. correlation of satisfaction results with other satisfaction indicators such as complaints and gains and losses of customers

d. how information on key products and service quality features that determine customer preference is extracted from customer satisfaction data

e. how customer satisfaction information is used in quality improvement

f. process used to evaluate and improve methods for determining customer satisfaction

7.7 Customer Satisfaction Results *(50 pts.)*

Briefly summarize trends in the company's customer satisfaction and in indicators of adverse customer response.

AREAS TO ADDRESS

a. trends in customer satisfaction and key customer satisfaction indicators for products and services segmented by customer groups, if appropriate

b. trends in major adverse indicators such as complaints, claims, refunds, mandatory recalls, returns, repeat services, replacements, downgrades, repairs, warranty costs and warranty work. Briefly explain adverse trends or data points.

Notes: *(1) Adverse indicators to be summarized in this Item relate to actions initiated by customers or on behalf of customers such as by government agencies or other third parties. Trends in adverse indicators where the action, such as recall or repeat service, is initiated by the company itself should be included in Item 6.1.*

(2) If the company has received any sanctions under regulation or contract over the past three years, include such information in this Item. Briefly describe how sanctions were resolved or current status.

7.8 Customer Satisfaction Comparison *(50 pts.)*

Compare the company's customer satisfaction results and recognition with those of competitors which provide similar products and services.

AREAS TO ADDRESS

a. comparison of customer satisfaction results with industry averages, industry leaders and world leaders, or with other competitors in the company's key markets

b. surveys, competitive awards, recognition and ratings by independent organizations including customers. Briefly explain surveys, awards, recognition and ratings.

c. trends in gaining or losing customers. Briefly explain sources of gains and losses.

d. trends in gaining and losing market share relative to major competitors, domestic and foreign. Briefly explain significant changes in terms of quality comparisons.

ORDERING GUIDELINES

Individual Copies

Individual copies of the 1990 Application Guidelines are available free of charge from:

Malcolm Baldrige National Quality Award   Telephone: 301-975-2036
National Institute of Standards and Technology   Telefax: 301-948-3716
Gaithersburg, MD 20899

Bulk Orders

Multiple copies of the 1990 Application Guidelines may be ordered in packets of 10 from:

American Society for Quality Control   Toll-Free: 800-952-6587
Customer Service Department   in Wisconsin: 414-272-8575
310 W. Wisconsin Avenue   Telefax: 414-272-1734
Milwaukee, WI 53203

STANDARD INDUSTRIAL CLASSIFICATION (SIC) CODES

Manufacturing and Products

Code	Sector	Code	Sector
01	Agriculture-crops	27	Printing and publishing
02	Agriculture-livestock	28	Chemicals
08	Forestry	29	Petroleum refining
09	Fishing and hunting	30	Rubber and plastics
10	Metal Mining	31	Leather and leather products
12	Coal mining		
13	Oil and gas extraction	32	Stone/clay/glass/concrete products
14	Mineral quarrying		
15	General building contractors	33	Primary metal industries
16	Heavy construction contractors	34	Fabricated metal products
17	Special trade contractors	35	Machinery/computer equipment
20	Food products	36	Electrical/electronic equipment
21	Tobacco products		
22	Textile mill products	37	Transportation equipment
23	Apparel	38	Instruments/clocks/optical goods
24	Lumber and wood products		
25	Furniture and fixtures	39	Miscellaneous manufacturing
26	Paper and allied products		

Services

Code	Sector	Code	Sector
07	Agricultural services	60	Banking
40	Railroad transportation	61	Credit agencies
41	Local & interurban transport	62	Security & commodity brokers
42	Trucking and warehousing		
44	Water transportation	63	Insurance carriers
45	Air transportation	64	Insurance agents
46	Pipelines/except natural gas	65	Real estate
47	Transportation services	67	Holding & other investment offices
48	Communications		
49	Electric/gas/sanitary services	70	Hotels and lodging places
		72	Personal services
50	Wholesale trade/durable goods	73	Business services
		75	Auto repair and services
51	Wholesale trade/nondurable goods	76	Miscellaneous repair services
52	Retail building materials	78	Motion pictures
53	General merchandise stores	79	Amusement and recreation
54	Food stores	80	Health services
55	Auto dealers & service stations	81	Legal services
		82	Educational services
56	Apparel and accessory stores	83	Social Services
		84	Museum and art galleries
57	Furniture stores	86	Membership organizations
58	Eating and drinking places	87	Professional services
59	Miscellaneous retail	89	Miscellaneous services

1989 Award Recipients

"...all American firms benefit by having a standard of excellence to match and perhaps, one day, to surpass. For 1989 there can be no higher standard of quality management than those provided by the winners of the Malcolm Baldrige National Quality Award– Milliken & Company and Xerox (Business Products and Systems)..."

George Bush
November 2, 1989

Milliken & Company

Headquartered in Spartanburg, South Carolina, the 124-year-old privately-owned Milliken & Company has 14,300 "associates" employed primarily at 47 manufacturing facilities in the United States. Milliken's 28 businesses produce more than 48,000 different textile and chemical products — ranging from apparel fabrics and automotive fabrics to specialty chemicals and floor coverings. Annual sales exceed $1 billion.

In 1981, senior management implemented Milliken's Pursuit of Excellence (POE), a commitment to customer satisfaction that pervades all company levels. This pursuit has led to improvements in what most competitors had already considered an enviable record of quality and performance. Since the early 1980s, productivity has increased 42 percent.

Teams are a hallmark of the Milliken quality improvement process. In 1988, 1,600 Corrective Action Teams formed to address specific manufacturing or other internal business problems, 200 Supplier Action Teams worked to improve Milliken's relationships with its suppliers, and nearly 500 teams responded to the needs and aims of customers. Quality improvement measures are solidly based on factual information, contained in an array of standardized databases accessible from all Milliken facilities. Most manufacturing processes are under the scrutiny of real-time monitoring systems that detect errors and help pinpoint their causes. Milliken's successful push for quality improvement has allowed it to increase U.S. sales and enter foreign markets.

Xerox Business Products and Systems

In 1983, Xerox Business Products and Systems launched an ambitious quality improvement program to arrest its decline in a world market it had once dominated. Today, the company can once again claim the title of the industry's best in nearly all copier-product markets. The company, headquartered in Stamford, Connecticut, attributes the turnaround to its strategy of "leadership through quality." Through extensive data-collection efforts, Xerox Business Products and Systems knows what customers want in products and services. Planning of new products and services is based on detailed analyses of data organized in some 375 information management systems, of which 175 are specific to planning, managing, and evaluating quality improvement.

Benchmarking is highly developed at Xerox Business Products and Systems. In all key areas of product, service, and business performance, the company measures its achievement for each attribute and compares itself with the level of performance achieved by the world leader, regardless of industry.

Quality improvement and, ultimately, customer satisfaction are the job of every employee. Working with the Amalgamated Clothing & Textile Workers Union, the company ensures that workers are vested with considerable authority over day-to-day work decisions. Employees are expected to take the initiative in identifying and correcting problems that affect the quality of products or services.

Xerox Business Products and Systems employs 50,200 people at 83 U.S. locations. The company makes more than 250 types of document-processing equipment. U.S. sales exceeded $6 billion in 1988.

1988 Award Recipients

Globe Metallurgical Inc.
Motorola Inc.
Commercial Nuclear Fuel Division of Westinghouse Electric Corporation

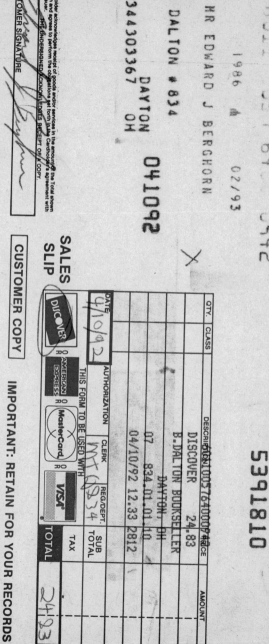

READER SURVEY

In order to make future editions of *Serving Them Right* more valuable to our readers, we are asking for your opinions. Please take a few minutes to tell us about the things you like or how the book might be improved. Thank you. Your answers are very much appreciated.

1. How much of the book did you have a chance to read?

   ☐ All of it
   ☐ Most of it
   ☐ Read some/parts of it
   ☐ Skimmed briefly
   ☐ Other:_____

2. Please rate the style or format of the book.

	Excellent	*Average*	*Improvement*
Well-organized			
Informative			
Easy to understand			
Helpful pictures and diagrams			
Right level of detail			
Good use of examples to illustrate ideas			

3. Which of the following topics did you find most or least valuable?

	Very Valuable				*Not Valuable*
Chapter One	5	4	3	2	1
Chapter Two	5	4	3	2	1
Chapter Three	5	4	3	2	1
Chapter Four	5	4	3	2	1
Chapter Five	5	4	3	2	1
Other:_____	5	4	3	2	1

4. Are there any topics or issues that were not adequately covered in the book?

☐ No

☐ Yes. What?_____

_____

5. How would you rate the book in terms of helping you improve customer-service levels at your company or job?

Very Helpful		*Not Helpful*	*Not Applicable*

10 9 8 7 6 5 4 3 2 1   0

6. What did you especially *like* about the book?

_____

_____

7. What did you especially *dislike* about the book or feel needed improvement?

_____

_____

8. How would you rate the book overall?

☐ Excellent
☐ Very Good
☐ Good
☐ Fair
☐ Poor

9. What is your professional title or work status? Please circle the appropriate letter in the list below:

A. Chairman/President/Owner/Partner
B. Vice President/Director/General Manager
C. Controller/Treasurer
D. Micro Manager/Specialist/Coordinator
E. Project Manager/Group Leader
F. Art Director/Graphic Designer/Artist/Illustrator
G. Manager/Supervisor (not listed above)
H. Architect/Engineer
I. Systems Analyst/Programmer

J. Consultant/Advisor

K. Scientist

L. Educator

M. Editor/Writer

N. Professional (Doctor, Lawyer)

O. Retired

P. Student

Q. Not Employed

R. Other:_____

10. What is your company's primary business activity? Please circle the appropriate letter in the list below:

A. Aerospace

B. Architecture, Engineering

C. Research and Development

D. Graphic Arts

E. Communications: Publishing, Advertising, Public Relations, Promotion

F. Government

G. Manufacturing

H. Education

I. Finance: Banking, Accounting, Insurance, Real Estate

J. Health, Medical, Legal

K. Retail, Wholesale, Distribution

L. Agriculture, Mining, Construction, Oil

M. Transportation, Utilities

N. Other (please specify)_____

O. Not applicable

Thank you for your opinions! Please send to:
Liswood Marketing Group
1932 1st Avenue
Suite 718
Seattle, WA,
98101